THE CRAFT
OF
Sermon
Construction

THE CRAFT
OF
Sermon
Construction

W. E. SANGSTER

A Pickering Classic

Originaly Published in 1954 by the Epworth Press
First published in 1978
by Pickering & Inglis,
3 Beggarwood Lane,
Baskingstoke, Hants RG23 7LP,
United Kingdom

First reissued in this format 1985

British Library Cataloguing in Publication

Sangster, William E.
    The craft of sermon construction.
    1. Preaching   2.Religious literature—
    Authorship
    I. Title
    251'.01   BV4211.1

    ISBN 0-7208-0404-4

Printed and bound in Great Britain by
Hunt Barnard Printing Ltd, Aylesbury, Bucks

This book has extended to a greater length than I expected or desired. . . . I, however, give thanks to God that with what little ability I possess I have . . . striven to depict, not the sort of man I am myself (for my defects are very many), but the sort of man he ought to be who desires to labour in sound . . . doctrine, not for his own instruction only, but for that of others also.

SAINT AUGUSTINE (354–430)

It is with no sense of having attained that I am to speak to you; for I always seem to myself to be only beginning to learn my trade; and the furthest I ever get in the way of confidence is to believe that I shall preach well next time.

JAMES STALKER (1848–1927)

Introduction

William Edwin Sangster (1900-1960)

The Craft of Sermon Construction

Great Britain, and America to a lesser extent, has not known a more compelling preacher than William Edwin Sangster. He served several churches in England before coming to his greatest ministry in the Westminster Central Hall in London, 1939-55, where in Methodism he was the scholar-evangelist of the pulpit. War demands, air raids, and living in shelters with people while writing a doctoral thesis and at the same time maintaining a full preaching schedule make him eminently qualified to write on what preaching should be.

His volumes of sermons show how his style was perfected and matured by the constant demands of preaching. The simplicity of speech, the choice of the right word, the urgency, the passionate concern for others, and the evangelistic spirit of this preacher permeate this volume. As he stated in Power in Preaching, "Doctrines must be preached practically and duties doctrinally." He set high standards for himself and thereby has given others a strong profile to emulate.

Much about the art of preaching can be learned from this book by a successful modern preacher. Preaching is not down-graded by this pulpit orator. On the contrary he maintains that preaching is still God's chief way of announcing His will to the world. Neither literature, broadcasting, counseling, movies, nor plays can displace preaching in the purpose of God. The preacher's valiant efforts to become what he should be must not be labeled as unimportant nor should they be regarded as futile. Preaching according to Sangster, did things — most important things. With such a guide who can fail to be inspired?

Everything about sermon construction is examined with perception and insight: the beginning, the conclusion, and how to prepare for preaching. No one can preach without preparing his own inner life. Sangster preached his most moving sermon as he lay dying slowly for a few years from an incurable disease. In that experience he touched more preachers by "the amassing of a great soul so as to have something worthwhile to give."

RALPH G. TURNBULL

Contents

Contents

I

A Plea for Preaching

PREACHING is in the shadows. The world does not believe in it. Perhaps it never did believe in it much, but it believed in it at one time more than it believes in it now.

This want of faith in Christian preaching on the part of men who make nothing of Christ ought not, of course, to surprise us. Why should they believe in it until they believe in him? The world's neglect, after all, may illustrate nothing but our own lack of those commanding figures who can so preach Christ that they compel the crowd to attend.

Or is there something deeper in it than that?

There are preachers who are drifting toward disbelief in preaching themselves. Indeed, some of them make no effort to disguise it. "I'm no entertainer," they say, with the sly insinuation that any man preaching to more than a handful must be employing some unworthy technique. "Thank God I'm no popular preacher!" say others, with the inverted vanity of those who want to imply that their preaching is not popular because it is so deep.

No men will receive respect for their calling who fail to respect it themselves.

Yet the diminishing faith in preaching among preachers themselves is not often so patent as that. Men are some-

times honestly unaware that confidence in their calling is
slipping from their minds. Though a man may be a minister of the Word, and sincerely believe himself called and
commissioned to preach, yet related occupations can work
themselves to the forefront of his thought and rob the
public proclamation of the gospel of its rightful priority
in all he does. False antitheses war at times in his heart,
and he may see things in opposition that God has joined
together and commands that no man put asunder.

What sad folly is it that has led ministers in many gen-
erations to see some innate controversy between preaching
and pastoral work? To make an either/or of this double
and related task is surely a suggestion of the devil. A man
in any normal ministerial situation, tempted to put the
emphasis on one of these tasks to the exclusion of the
other, might well listen to his Master's word: " This ought
ye to have done, and not to leave the other undone."

It would be hard to exaggerate all the gains to a preacher
from pastoral work faithfully done: the insight into people's minds; the awareness of problems which perplex
them and temptations which test them; the opportunity to
learn with intimacy from life — so necessary to a man
whose main learning is from books. Even if he were thinking most narrowly of the *preacher's* office and not of himself as a shepherd of souls, the minister could not fail to be
a true pastor of his flock.

But being a shepherd isn't the same as being a sheep dog!
Caring for people doesn't mean fussing around them in the
morning hours when a man should be in his study and on
his knees. Collecting a congregation by assiduous visiting,
but having no sure word from God when they come together in worship, is only to disappoint the expectations
one has aroused, and to fail in a task so solemn and exalted
that no part of our duty can exceed its importance.

If it is a false antithesis to place preaching and pastoral work in opposition, what shall we say of those who deal similarly with preaching and the conduct of worship, or preaching and the observance of Holy Communion? Liturgiology has displaced preaching in the interests of many who minister in holy things. "Worship is so much more than preaching," they say, and the fact that superficially the statement is not only true but platitudinous must not blind us to the deep falsity that lies at its heart. Others say, "It is our high privilege to celebrate the Holy Eucharist: nothing else matters." The same false antithesis appears here also.

The taproot of this deep error is a low view of preaching. It is not seen as a sacramental act. It is thought of as a man talking, sharing his own views, making his own comments. On such a view of preaching, a sermon and an address are synonymous. In point of fact, they are nothing of the sort. Give the words their strict meaning and an address is a man talking to men; a sermon is a man speaking *from God*. The authority of the preacher, unlike that of a speaker, is not in himself: he is a herald. His word is not his own; it comes from above.

Nor is this deep difference denied, even though it be proved by common usage that a sermon and an address are regarded as the same thing — sometimes, unhappily, by preachers themselves.

That only illustrates again how poor a view of preaching prevails in many quarters — and some of them ecclesiastical — and accounts in part for the disregard that preaching suffers in the world today. The difference between an address and a sermon is deep, basic, elemental. Any preacher who knows his business knows the difference *in himself*. He is ready, of course, when occasion demands, to give a religious address. He may even give an address now and then from the pulpit. But always he feels on such occasion that this is not preaching. It is not "the sacrament of the Word." He would prefer to be on a platform, and he wants to say with Paul that on this occasion he is not expounding the Word, for he has no special revelation from the Lord, but is giving only the fruit of his own thinking.

It is not hard to prove that this high view of preaching was held by the Protestant Reformers. Men were ordained, in their view, to the ministry *of the Word* and the sacraments. Both! Both together!

Setting preaching and worship in opposition, or disparaging the ministry of the Word in the foolish supposition that it exalts the celebration of the Eucharist, would have seemed blasphemous to them. Indeed, they placed the sermon at that point in the service where the deepest solemnities of the Mass had previously been observed. The sermon became "the monstrance of the Evangel." What they still believed to be true of the blessed sacrament of His broken body and spilt blood they cherished in their cultus, but they recognized in *preaching* something infinitely more sublime than a man's comment on the lesson for the day, or "a few thoughts that have occurred to me during the week," or "a little advice which I hope will do you good."

Preaching, in Bernard Manning's phrase, was "a manifestation of the Incarnate Word, from the written Word, by the spoken word." Properly understood, it is that still. It is a showing forth of the reigning Christ. It is an assault upon the gates of hell, and, indeed, a piercing of them. It is a deed, not of man merely or chiefly, but of God.

Let preaching be so understood and it is plain at once that to place preaching and worship in opposition is more than foolish: it is surely nonsense. The practice in some churches for members of the congregation to leave before the sermon begins, on the theory that worship is over and what remains is just a man giving his view on certain matters (which may be no better views than their own), reveals more plainly than anything else the low view of preaching we are contesting here. The fact that the preacher himself understands their action and concurs in it does not prove that they are right. It proves that he also is wrong. It explains why he may scamp his own preparation for preaching — treat it, indeed, as an unimportant addendum of the service — and regret the expectations of those " uninstructed " members of his flock who persist in hoping that in the sermon also they will meet God.

If it be said in response to all this that we are taking a view of preaching so high and awful that any man might well shrink from it — most especially if he be a layman serving as local preacher or lay reader — the inference need not be resisted. It *is* a high and awful task from which any man might well shrink. That is why the Church in its wisest hours has always insisted that a man must have a divine call to it. The work cannot be sustained on anything less. Men have begun the work just as an occupation, a way of earning their bread. A man may, indeed, enjoy it in his early days at no higher level than that. If he has facility in public speech and it satisfies the tendency to exhibitionism which is in us all, he may, for a while, be content.

But only for a while! He cannot *sustain* a ministry that way. The scorn or chill indifference of the world will freeze him. The pleasure he derives from self-display passes the point of satiety. The middle years come and mock his early enjoyment at hearing himself talking, and nothing can keep him going with real devotion if he cannot look back and say to himself, " *I was called.*"

One thing, if he is wise, he will be most careful *not* to

do: he will not force into ungodly opposition things that
God has joined together. Preaching and worship belong
to one another. However personally unworthy he knows
himself to be, he knows also that, having called him to the
work, God is pledged to meet his faithfulness with the
Holy Spirit and speak through him. He will not magnify
himself, but he *will* magnify his office. Treating it with
awful seriousness himself, he knows that men will not be
able cheerfully to ignore him. Howsoever they come within
reach of his voice, if, indeed, he is God's messenger, the
message will pierce their minds and challenge their wills.
They may ignore the challenge and turn away from the
truth, but they will go away as the rich young ruler went
away — sorrowful. Indeed, it is only their bodies that they
will carry away; their hearts will run after the Lord, whose
voice they have heard in the voice of his faithful servant.

No one who takes this high view of preaching could ever
think of it as entertainment. He could as soon regard the
Holy Table made ready for those that do " truly and ear-
nestly repent " of their sins as a piece of " showmanship."

Nor will anyone who takes this high view of preaching
be seriously troubled by those who complain that it is *too*
high; that a man holding it makes too much of preaching.
He can never make enough of it! If, indeed, it were only
a display of his own gifts and his own ideas, he would
deserve their rebukes, but would a prophet allow a priest
to tell him that he had received no message from God or
suffer himself to be lectured on his lack of humility because
he began by declaring: " Thus saith the Lord "?

Let those whose chief service to religion is to make real
to others the value of liturgies do their work to the glory
of God and all will be blessed, but let them hesitate to im-
pute meaner motives to other men and subtly imply that
their own work is the pure worship of God while communions that put great stress on preaching can be only delight-

ing in the refined entertainment value of men with oratorical gifts.

It borders on the blasphemous so to describe " the manifestation of the Incarnate Word, from the written Word, by the spoken word." Surely — if one put it no higher than this — it cannot be more worshipful to offer one's petitions to God than to hear his Word proclaimed. Our wishes cannot be more devout than his will. Nor does it seem possible that anything could more move a sluggish soul to adoration than the presentation of God's timeless truth and the forceful reminder of his manifold mercies. The most solemn symbols of the faith — if only because of their familiarity and because they are material signs — are limited in their ability to convey the grace and truth of God.

If a man entertains a low view of preaching himself, let him, at least, be careful not to ascribe it to others. Let him differ from his fellow Christians if he must, but let him see what they are seeking and judge them at their best. He may note their failures to reach their own ideal (of which many of them are keenly aware themselves!), but he must not mistake their aim or caricature their purpose. Not by accident, nor yet by the thrustful egotism of men, was the pulpit given the central place in the Reformed Churches. It is there of design and devotion. It is there by the logic of things. It is there as " *the throne of the Word of God.*"

Nothing would do more to recover a sense of the greatness of preaching than truly to recognize what preaching really is and to see it integrated with worship itself. It will make a preacher say, " It is high; I cannot attain unto it," but his conscious incapacity will bring him where God wants him to be, for when he is weak then is he strong.

We have seen, so far, that preaching suffers depreciation when it is forced into a false antithesis with pastoral work and with the conduct of worship, but we have said that it suffers also when related occupations rob it of its due priority in the ministerial life.

What are these " related occupations "?

Academic research is one. The preacher must be, to the extent of his abilities and opportunities, a scholar, but it is easily possible with men of academic tastes for research to cease to be the servant of the pulpit and become its rival. Absorbed in some byway of history or literature, a man can forget that the purpose of study in the life of the preacher is to make him better able to expound the Word of God and that, no matter how simple he may judge his congregation to be, the adequate service of his people will take all the time he has.

It is always dangerous for a man to despise — however secretly — the intelligence of those to whom he ministers. For one thing, he cannot keep it secret. In subtle ways he betrays himself, and if the people are not resentful, they are hurt. The simplest people can take the best we have to give. It just requires not less but more time to get it ready: to make it plain, vivid, understandable. Their gratitude to one who will take that trouble is beautiful indeed.

If anyone doubts the danger to ministers of becoming preoccupied with academic research, let him note the subjects on which some men ordained to preach the Word of God spend years of study in the preparation of a thesis for a higher university degree. With the best will in the world, it is hard to believe, on looking at some of the subjects, that, in being separated to holy things, they were separated to do that.

The work of the psychological clinic becomes a rival to the pulpit in the minds of other men. Admiring and half envying the skill a psychologist may possess to put his finger on the hidden need in someone's tangled life, and sensing the relationship that this has with ministerial work, they take it up and find that it absorbs more time than they thought.

Not content to confine themselves to " counseling," and being unwilling to direct people whose need they suspect to a professional psychologist who is a Christian too, they attempt the hard task of practicing two professions.

Both suffer! — though it is the harm to their pulpit work that concerns us most here. That one or two ministers have had conspicuous success in both offices should not betray their smaller imitators into anticipating a similar result.

Undoubtedly the offices of pastor and Christian psychologist are sister callings. A minister is often, by the very nature of his work, the first to sense people's need of professional counsel. If he is a good enough psychologist himself to divine the areas of their trouble, let him use his knowledge to direct them where those needs can be met, but let him beware of setting up as a psychoanalyst himself. It is a time-devouring occupation and still leaves the harder task of psychosynthesis to be done. He has been ordained to preach the Word, minister the sacraments, shepherd the flock. If he is *really* doing it well, it will take all his time.

Youth clubs, church "institutes," community centers, and marriage guidance clinics filch the time of other good men from pulpit preparation. As good a case can be made out for these as for the other related occupations that elbow the proclamation of the Word of God from the forefront of a man's mind. In some areas men feel that it is the only way to make contact with the neighborhood. "Sunday is not the chief day in our week," they say, and the dwindling handful that gathers for worship confirms this. A man's strength may go, therefore, into club activities, socials, dances, dramatics, pie suppers, operettas, but it works round in a vicious circle. He exhausts himself in these activities (and sometimes ruefully admits that he can find no real " tie-up " between them and the Church of God!), comes to his preaching ill-prepared and physically below par, and the loyal handful, finding no nourishment in what he brings on Sunday, grows sadly smaller still.

Some men seem to know how to relate these social activities to spiritual things. I suspect that they do so by keeping them firmly in their subordinate place. I believe that they fence off in every week solid hours for pulpit preparation, and that their people know — be they few or not so few — that whenever they come to worship they will come to food.

It is no narrow view of the ministerial office that is being expounded here. Here is no covert plea that a man do nothing but preach. But it *is* a protest against the view which seems to be gaining ground, that a minister is a man who does everything *except* preach. And by " preach " I do not mean fill fifteen or twenty minutes in public worship with certain thoughts that have come to him in a bus queue, but rather the utterance of a man who knows himself called of God to proclaim His Word; who, with religious firmness, gives the best hours of every week to prayerful work upon the Scriptures; and who mounts his pulpit steps on Sunday knowing that he has a message from the Lord. Because — let there be no doubt about it — this was, is, and ever will be God's chief way of announcing his will to the world.

Some people have expressed the opinion that preaching has no natural supremacy in God's intention, but appears to possess it only because, in the first century, it was the one means possible of publishing a message abroad. Printing was not yet invented. Radio and the cinema were not even thought of. The only way, therefore, that a message could be given was by men going from place to place and speaking of it (though κήρυγμα cannot be confined, of course, to *public* speech). Hence the oral gospel preceded the written gospel. The whole progress of the cause of God depended upon it then. When Paul said, "How shall they hear without a preacher?" it was a rhetorical question. It expected no answer. In the first century men could hear in no other way.

"They could now!" say some. "There are better ways of publicizing the faith than by preaching. Books and newspapers go into families the members of which never go to church. Broadcast religion reaches an audience immeasurably wider than the unaided human voice. Christianity could be presented in moving pictures and move an audience more mightily than the most eloquent speaker. Isn't it a little archaic to suppose that preaching must ever be (after the witness of a holy life) the chief way of spreading the faith?"

It is *not* archaic. Radio religion is still a man preaching, his audience vastly increased, it is true, and his personality necessarily muffled to some extent by the very device that splashes his words across a continent. That books and the cinema have been an aid to religion — and could be greater aids — none can doubt, but can either of them, or both together, be a substitute for a Spirit-filled man looking men in the face and speaking the Word of God to their consciences and hearts?

The very logic of the communication proves it. A personal God, seeking the love and fellowship of persons, seeks best by a person speaking direct to persons. The message is mediated, it is true, but nearer one could not get to immediate communion, short of intimate communion with God in one's heart. Read a speech of the most moving orator, and how poor it is in comparison with the same words heard as they fell from his lips! One gets his meaning, but not *him*. Only half of him comes over the air when he broadcasts; less than half through the screen.

The work of the preacher, as he expounds the written Word to his congregation, must ever be the supreme method of God's communication with men. Other means may aid this method, but nothing can supplant it. If our lot is cast in an age with little more than amused contempt for preaching, that in no way affects its importance or its pre-eminence in the purpose of God. Christ came preaching. From the Day of Pentecost, the apostles spent themselves in preaching. Great movements in the Church have normally been initiated and developed by preaching. Revival has invariably come by preaching. By preaching, it may confidently be anticipated, it will come again.

Let us not confuse the difficulties of it, or men's apparent lack of taste for the work even when it is done, with its importance. To fly from the preacher's task because it is hard or unappreciated is, for any man who has received Christ's commission or to whom He proffers it, something near to apostasy. For every reason that can appeal to the mind and heart of a consecrated man, the call to preach, if it has come to him, must be answered with all that he has. If, having answered the call long ago, he finds his zeal abating with the years, let him examine his heart to learn how this loss of faith came about.

The reasons are often quite personal. Some men have half-unconsciously lost faith in the message itself and in its ability to meet the need of the world in any wide way. What relevance has evangelism, they ask, in an age that toys with atomic bombs? Having lost faith in the message, how can they have passion in its proclamation? Other men have grown weary of offering what so few seem to want. They have said that Christ is utterly necessary to the full life, but the multitude pass unheeding by and get on apparently quite happily without him. Only those who have had the experience know how depressing it can be to pour out one's soul to a small company of people which never seems to grow, and never seems much affected by what is said. If a man in those circumstances does not guard with jealous care his periods of daily devotion, his work becomes a dull routine. Nothing ever happens, and — worse still — he no longer thinks it will.

Because the company that comes to hear the gospel is small, and either has embraced the Truth or never will embrace it, a minister may begin to make scanty preparation. A few unrelated thoughts are offered in place of a sermon. He repeats himself, and not in the fresh way the gospel must ever be repeated, but boringly. Inevitably, the few get even fewer.

Still other men have convinced themselves that able preaching all depends on the possession of certain special gifts which, with modesty, they confess they do not possess themselves. The absence of those gifts does not move them (as their congregation might suppose) to harder work that the deficiency might be made up, but serves as an excuse for wearying the people without any pangs of conscience. Clearly, the blame is God's because he was grudging with the gifts!

It cannot be denied, of course, that there *are* special aptitudes for the task, though the God who called can be trusted to equip. If the man of modest gifts places his five barley loaves and two small fish on the altar, who dares to deny that, even with them, God may feed a multitude?

The quite personal reasons that lead preachers themselves to lose faith in preaching do not end even here. Some men with a love of their calling belong to an itinerant ministry, and lose heart because of the lack of " concentration " in preaching. The power of preaching, they believe, depends in part on its consecutiveness — the same man speaking to the same congregation week after week. A ministerial situation that keeps them constantly " on the wing " inwardly frets some of the most earnest men, and they fail of their best because — mistakenly — they feel that the circumstances do not call for it. Lay preachers, whose work normally provides no " concentration " at all, sometimes feel the same frustration.

Let any young preacher troubled by thoughts of this character remember that a lack of full concentration in his early years may be a blessing. Fewer sermons should mean better sermons. Better sermons will mean, in due course, all the concentration he desires.

Called to preach! That is the basic thing at the last. Let a man be sure of that, and keep his certitude by obedience, and he will have the answer to all the doubts that dog the steps of a preacher regarding his vocation.

Commissioned of God to teach the Word! A herald of the great King! A witness of the eternal gospel! Could any work be more high and holy? To this supreme task God sent his only begotten Son. In all the frustration and confusion of the times, is it possible to imagine a work comparable in importance with that of proclaiming the will of God to wayward men?

Only a divine commission can justify it. Lacking that, it is a gross impertinence. No humble man would take upon himself the task of talking to others in a public place about the most intimate things of the soul.

Perhaps that is why a normal man resents the mention of religion by a stranger and regards as impudent any inquiry on an unexpected occasion concerning his relationships with God. "Who gave you the right," he seems to say, " to put that question to me? "

Searching preaching is either divinely inspired or intolerably insolent. What but a warrant from God could justify one mortal in provoking, probing, piercing the consciences of others . . . and in public, too! (No man worthy of respect ever preaches accusingly at one selected person in his congregation. When he knows in his soul that he must utter a word of rebuke to an individual, he does so to him alone.)

Yet there is a terrible personalness about *general* preaching at times. Uttered in honesty to all, it has power to break congregations into units and leave each one aware (like John Henry Newman) "of two and two only absolute and luminously self-evident beings": himself and his Creator.

No other form of human address is like this. It is, indeed, one way in which the Word of God authenticates itself. That is why the preacher may boldly say at times: "If this word of mine is not confirmed in your consciences by the Spirit of God, and nothing inside you says, '*This is true*,' disregard it." Who with a shred of modesty in his soul and smartingly aware that he is a sinner himself would charge, challenge, and affront his fellows in that way? Only a man who knows himself divinely appointed so to do!

The divine origin of the message is not proved only by the vulnerability of conscience to it. It is proved also by the things that preaching does.

Nothing is more foolish in connection with this subject than the supposition that preaching does not *do* anything. Preaching is a constant agent of the divine power by which the greatest miracle God ever works is wrought and wrought again. God uses it *to change lives*. It is hard for any mortal to tell, either of himself or of others, what forces have worked upon him to issue in some dramatic change of life, but many affirm that the occasion, and no small part of the cause, was *one* sermon. It would be wearisome to set out the names even of the most notable of those who have conspicuously served God and who traced the real beginnings of their life of surrender and service to meeting him while a man preached. Looked at in one way, a sermon is a most impermanent thing. Hours of deep brooding, honest study, and not a little prayer . . . and it is gone with the wind. Looked at in another way, it partakes of eternity. Quite literally, the force of some sermons will never end.

When Wilfred Grenfell went to hear the Studd brothers preach, his mind was already half inclined to abandon the Christian faith altogether. He heard, and thereupon determined " to make religion a real effort to do as I thought Christ would do in my place." [1] All Labrador was blessed by that sermon. Grenfell's example has inspired millions. In ever-widening circles, the influence of that inspiriting word goes on and on.

The power of preaching is not, however, confined to occasions when a life is dramatically changed. More often it concerns itself with teaching and feeding the faithful; or giving comfort to those wounded in the battle, or courage to those wanting to quit the field, or strength to those hard pressed by temptation.

What an unspeakable privilege to be allowed and equipped by God to do such lovely work! When one thinks of the awful wounds life administers at times — the sudden bereavements and betrayals, the secret anxieties and the gnawing inner griefs — to be able to speak a *sure* word of God to suffering souls is an honor of which no man is truly worthy.

[1] *A Labrador Doctor, the Autobiography of Sir Wilfred T. Grenfell*, p. 31. Hodder & Stoughton, Ltd.

But does it not call for all a man has of heart and mind and will? Daunting as the task is, is it not plain that a man, being called and knowing God is faithful, is summoned to whole-souled consecration? Shoddy work in any calling is unworthy, but in *this* calling it would be blasphemous too.

No related occupation can squeeze this task from its central place. No personal fad, or mood of self-pity, should blind a man to the greatness of his work.

If he comes to it aware of his awful privilege and open to the endowments which God gives to those he calls, his church may not fill, but his people will be blessed. " Always we get bread," they will say: " morning and evening, in May and November, if he expects a crowd or only a handful — always the same thorough preparation, always bread! "

Such a man will not lack hearers. The rumor of his faith-fulness and God's power will go abroad, and the hungry sheep will gather and be fed.

Because — despite all the evidence to the contrary — people both need and want the Word of God.

Who can doubt it?

A dependable word about heaven in the atomic age! Peace of heart in a world filled with the threat of war! Love for hate, joy for tears, power for impotence!

Nobody but the preacher (and a few philosophers maybe) even pretend to answer the questions that men in their moments of starkest honesty most desire to have met: Who am I? Why am I here? What is the meaning of life? Is there life after death? What is the truth of the world? Is there a God? Can I be sure?

Oddly enough, despite their superficial resentment of any mention of their sins (and their denial at times that they have any!), men do not seriously respect a preacher who does not cut into their consciences and make them know that in a sermon they are meeting God and not just hearing another mortal pour out his unimportant thoughts. They cannot always put the difference they feel into words. "He does not get beneath my skin," they say — and leave it there. Discussion as to whether we want less or more preaching is sterile. Better preaching is our need.

It is estimated in round figures that fifty thousand sermons are preached in England and Wales every Sunday, and five to six times that number in the United States of America. In an age when it is freely said that religion is decaying in the Western world those figures should be given their full force. What other subject could sustain such constant exposition and discussion, or continue to receive a hearing, or prove — when preaching is at its best —so simultaneously stimulating and inexhaustible? Such concentration on politics would make politics completely repugnant. Such emphasis on physical health would make people literally ill.

Only the Word of God can abide such mining, for only the Word of God has such ore to yield.

It would be foolish — and worse — to suppose that because this work is divine in its origin there is no technique to study and no craft to learn. The history of preaching records no sadder story than that of those misguided zealots who have brought no consecration of mind to the preaching of the Word and have just "opened their mouth" in public in expectation that the Spirit would do the rest. The Spirit spurns their superstitious sloth.

For every reason that can appeal to faithful and rational men this task demands that we be master craftsmen.

To the study of the craft of sermon construction, therefore, let us now turn.

II

Sermons Classified According to Subject Matter

WE CONCLUDED the previous chapter by admitting that some preachers feel no need at all of help in the craft of sermon-making. "The apostles received no such instruction," they say. "They depended entirely upon the Holy Spirit. So do we!" If some public success has attended their early and uninstructed efforts, they are confirmed in their independence of human help. They may even flatter themselves that they do better than the people who have had expert direction.

This book is not for them. If their speaking is largely limited to personal testimony, and has never been put to the stern test of talking twice a Sunday to the same people for ten years, they can go on and do, perhaps, a useful work in their simple way.

But it is foolish and, indeed, blasphemous of them to suggest that the Holy Spirit objects to hard work. The contrary is the case. The divine Paraclete delights in blessing those who prove their consecration by their own incessant toil. "The plus of the Spirit" is given to him of whom it can be said, "He has done what he could."

The craft of sermon construction is, in some ways, like the study of logic. One learns no new fact. The gains appear in a sounder judgment and a profoundly different approach to the work.

No well-trained speaker, on the eve of making a speech, assembles in his mind all that he knows of logic and, with a constant reference to the rules of argument, begins to set his thoughts down.

Not a bit of it! The logical discipline has gone into him somewhere. In making his speech, he is concerned only with the lucid expression of what is in his mind, and how (if the speech is propagandist) he can persuade others to share his view. For the most part, his logical discipline works unconsciously. When he reads his speech over before its delivery, some subtle fallacy may leap to his eye and he will see more swiftly than other men the weak links in the argument, but, for the most part, the gains of his iron mental discipline are not easily tabulated.

But they are there! The order, progression, and structural soundness of what the speaker has to say are all in debt to a study that taught him no new fact, and the technical terms of which he often forgets himself, but a study that has made him an undisputed member of the rare order of thinkers.

So with preachers who study the craft of sermon construction. They will never begin the preparation of a sermon by assembling all that they know of the theory of homiletics, and start by pouring their teeming thoughts into this mold or that. The study will sink into them and at times (even to themselves) be lost to view.

But all their work will bear the fine impress of that discipline (if, indeed, it has been honestly borne), and just as there is weight and power, even to uncultured minds, in a fine argument logically sound, so to a congregation composed even of the tinker, tailor, soldier, sailor, there is an awareness of being in the hands of a master craftsman when the Word of God is expounded by one who understands his task. He, of all men, knows the element of falsity in the common phrase that "preaching can't be taught."

The theory of this thing matters even though it is not taught to be remembered. When it has become a subconscious habit, it can be forgotten. He can conceive and gestate and deliver his sermon without any conscious reference to the theory of homiletics at all. But, as a craftsman, he will be forever better for the serious apprenticeship that he has served.

A sermon has been variously defined, and the definition that we have adopted here is Bernard Manning's: "A manifestation of the Incarnate Word, from the written Word, by the spoken word." It will seem a less accurate definition of some forms of preaching than of others, but it keeps the emphasis in the right place. It draws with firmness the distinction between preaching and all other forms of public address. A sermon is not a lecture, because its aim is not simply to inform. It is not a platform speech, because it is not the delivery of one man's thoughts to others. It is nearer the work of a herald, yet with this important difference: a herald today is *merely* a mouthpiece, and a preacher when he preaches must give himself.

Sermons can be classified in various ways. They can be classified by:

1. Their subject matter — the actual content of the sermon.
2. Their central structure — the sheer architecture of their building.
3. The psychological method employed in their presentation — the way of "putting it over."

The first classification concerns us now, and the other two will occupy us in subsequent chapters.

The classification of sermons according to their subject

matter has often been undertaken by writers on homiletics, and there is a grouping now that can almost be called " classical."

It runs (with some variations) like this:

    I. Biblical Interpretation.
   II. Ethical and Devotional.
  III. Doctrinal.
  IV. Philosophic and Apologetic.
   V. Social.
  VI. Evangelistic.

This classification is not so sharp that one type cannot merge into others. Indeed, as I have stated, some able teachers of homiletics scorn the classification entirely. No sermon is a Christian sermon at all, they say, that is not based on the Bible; ethical, therefore, in its nature, and evangelistic in its appeal. They continue to doubt whether this kind of classification helps us at all.

I think it does!

It is true that most good sermons, on being expertly examined, will be found to include elements of three or even four of these types, but it is true, nonetheless, that they are likely to belong to one group in the main. In any case, the types are clearly distinguishable *in thought*. A characteristic example of one kind would not be confused with a characteristic example of another. Each is a true type of preaching. They overlap. Happily, no type has edges so clean-cut that it refuses relations with the others. When we come to define what we mean by each in turn, it will be found, I believe, that every legitimate kind of preaching has been covered here.

Yet before we turn to closer definition a final objection must be met. Some preachers are so enamored of one kind of preaching, and so equipped by study and temperament to employ it, that they tend to deny the legitimacy of all others. "No preaching is preaching that is not plain Biblical interpretation," say some. "The only preaching worth the name," say others, "is evangelistic." "Stick to doctrine," says a third group. "Our great need is not exhortation but teaching."

Nor do the partisans end even here. Still others say, "We live in an age of overwhelming social concerns: social preaching is the clamant need of the hour."

And — as is so often true when men argue — they are *all* right in their affirmations and wrong only in their denials. We say again that each of the groups we have distinguished is a true type of preaching. A man may be much more seized by the importance of one type than of another and strongly feel that he has a special call to work that way.

Let him so work! — but let him beware of two things: first, of excommunicating those who work as devoutly in another segment of the field, and, secondly, of wearying his congregation by an unvarying approach to that many-faceted thing that we call truth.

Biblical interpretation apart, each of these types of preaching could become sadly monotonous if it were the only kind a patient congregation ever heard.

Nor would the *monotony* be the chief peril. Preoccupation with any one of these sermon types (Biblical interpretation again excepted) means that many important aspects of truth are being disregarded. That *does* matter! The diet would not be balanced, and any dietitian knows, in these days when vitamins are so closely studied, that an unbalanced diet imperils health.

Let us turn, then, to a closer scrutiny of each of these types of preaching that we have distinguished. The classification of sermons according to subject matter has not

been (in our view) superseded. It has theoretical value
still. For the purposes of clear thought, the classification
makes *necessary* distinctions. While it is true that "topical preaching" and "life-situation preaching" (at both of
which we must look later) are more popular definitions of
sermon craft, and cut clean across the older classification,
they have not really superseded the distinctions that the
centuries have found of use.

We begin, as we must, with the Bible.

I. Biblical Interpretation

Our definition of a sermon stated that it was "a manifestation of the Incarnate Word, *from the written Word,*
by the spoken word."

"From the written Word"! It is all based on the Bible.
Whether it is true to say that the Bible *is* the Word of God,
or whether, as some believe, it is only accurate to say that
the Bible *contains* the Word of God, we will not pause
now to discuss. It is common ground with all Christians
that the Bible is the supreme "source book" of our faith,
and that in all the literature of the world it is not first in a
category, but occupies a category alone. In the exact sense
of that much misused word, it is *unique*. It holds the authoritative record of our religion. It tells, as no other book
does (not even the holy books of other faiths), the story
of God's dealing with man, and man's experience of God.
It contains not only the story of God's unfolding of himself in the centuries before Christ, but the only authentic
record of the life of Christ.

There are legitimate forms of Christian preaching (so
we have argued) that are not direct expositions of the
Bible, but no preaching that is out of harmony with the
Bible, and no preaching that cannot honestly be related to

the Bible, can establish its claim to be Christian preaching at all.

If, of the various types of preaching that we have classified, the preacher were compelled to confine himself to one, it would be this. No classification of preaching comes nearer to universality. By preaching through the Bible, and applying it to modern life, the preacher could cover (either directly or by implication) nearly every human need.

Recent scholarship has deeply affected modern views of the Bible. It is almost certain that we understand the Scriptures in some ways better than they were ever understood before, for researches into the original tongues, the analysis of the various books, and the knowledge of nations contemporaneous with the Hebrews have shed floods of light on much that was previously obscure in the Book of God.

But the Bible does not reveal its deepest message to the secular littérateur, nor even to the student of Greek minutiae as such, and still less to those who come to it with theories they want to prove. It gives its treasure to those who have spiritual insight, and it is the simple truth to say that some with the widest knowledge of Greek particles and of the contemporary literary background lack that spiritual insight, and that some possess the insight who know nothing of J, E, P, and D, and would not understand what a man meant if he raised a question concerning the Synoptic problem.

How to retain what is truly valuable in the gains of recent scholarship and yet to recover the awesome reverence for the Bible that our fathers possessed is one of the great problems facing the modern preacher.

But this is sure, whenever preaching is devout Biblical

interpretation: It gives *authority* to the spoken word. Never is the preacher more a herald than when he is down hard upon the Book; never is it plainer that the word which he speaks is not his own but Another's.

Moreover, Biblical interpretation provides *endless material* for the preacher. Some men, whose range in preaching does not include Biblical interpretation, "run out of gospel." They exhaust the topics on which they have anything to say. They waste precious hours every week finding a theme. The Bible preacher, on the other hand, is embarrassed by his riches. His subjects form a queue demanding to be heard.

The Biblical interpreter gains here also. He is *kept on guard against his own bias.* Most preachers have a few favorite themes and a few pet aversions. Half unaware of it themselves, they stress their own interests to the point of being wearisome. A man preaching regularly on the Bible (and not simply *from* it) has an extra safeguard against the pull of personal interest. His themes are as fresh as the Bible is fresh, and the Bible is new every morning.

Furthermore, systematic Bible preaching has this precious by-product: *it encourages the people who hear it to read the Bible for themselves.* The preacher's own unflagging interest in the Book incites an interest in others. What the minister finds so fascinating, the people rightly suppose will have its fascination for themselves. They turn to it, therefore, and feed on what they find.

Nor do the gains end even here. There are difficult themes which demand attention in the pulpit, but which any man, personally acquainted with the people in the pews, might be tempted to neglect: e.g., divorce, the best use of Sunday, temperance, dubious pleasures, the judgments and punishments of God.

A Bible preacher *cannot dodge the difficult.* As he works

through a Gospel or Epistle, he comes to the "hard sayings." They *must* be faced.

If the progression of his Bible exposition had not brought him to them, and he had selected a subject seemingly at random and in the disconnected way that topical preaching invites, he might be suspected of pointing his dart specifically at someone in the pew known to be needing a particular message and to whom it is painfully applicable.

Consecutive Bible interpretation secures him from that suspicion. It makes the awkward theme natural, and enables him to cover aspects of truth from which, by inclination, he would shrink.

Putting all these gains together, therefore, the primacy of Biblical interpretation in preaching is fully made out, and some might wonder why any other classification of sermons (so far as subject matter is concerned) is really called for.

These reasons call for them:

People do not believe in the Bible as once they did. I am not now thinking of the different attitudes toward Biblical criticism within the Church of God, but the attitude toward the Bible of people outside the Church. Time was when a man who utterly ignored the Church had still an inherited reverence for the Bible as the Word of God, and could be challenged with effectiveness on its authority. That day has largely gone. Masses of people now believe that the Bible is a bundle of "outworn Jewish rags." Some think that it was all an invention of priests to keep the poor in their places. The apposite citation of a Scripture text in argument today may create more amusement than conviction.

Nor does the Bible ever set out in an overt way to "prove" itself. It is true that it proves itself in subtle ways to any man's conscience who will open himself to its

influence. But it is never self-conscious about it: never
marshals a set of arguments to put it beyond doubt that
it is, indeed, the Word of God.

The Bible never seeks to prove the existence of God, or
the efficacy of prayer, or man's moral freedom, or his sur-
vival of death.

It *assumes* all these basic facts of the religious life — but,
frankly, the modern preacher cannot assume them, certainly not with a congregation that includes unbelievers.
Hence the need for preaching that we have classified as
philosophic and apologetic — preaching that begins earlier,
in a sense, than the Bible itself begins.

Nor does the Bible deal in any *direct* way with many
ethical and social problems that press upon a man of sensitive conscience today. Does the New Testament teach us
with unmistakable plainness how a modern State, nomi-
nally Christian, should deal with a powerful neighbor
aggressively atheistic and undisguisedly militant? The Old
Testament, in certain parts, might seem to give authority
for slaughtering them. But the *New?*

Does the Bible put beyond all question a Christian's
attitude to birth control, capital punishment, palaces for
bishops, nationalization of the mines, eugenics, total ab-
stinence from alcoholic drink, social credit, emigration
quotas, interest on loans, and tariff barriers? A hundred
other similarly urgent problems could as easily be set
down.

If it is answered that all these problems are dealt with
in principle in the Bible, the principle must be at least a
little obscure if only because Christians themselves (who
all acknowledge the authority of the Book) continue to
argue about them.

If, on the other hand, it is considered unreasonable to
expect a plain answer from the Book to the pressing prob-

lems of every succeeding generation, no more need be said.

It is our concern at the moment only to establish this: that while Biblical interpretation must ever be the first category in our classification of sermons arranged according to subject matter, it is not, as some contend, the *only* category. The sweep of Christian preaching will never carry us beyond the sphere of Bible interest, but it will carry us beyond immediate Bible exposition. The primary place in preaching, of course, will always be given to work on the Book. A link with the Bible will normally be found even in a chain that seems to lead us away from it. But the man who says that no preaching is Christian preaching that is not direct Bible interpretation has overstated his case.

It will comfort us in telling him so to remember that Jesus was no Bible preacher in *his* sense of the word. He expounded the Scriptures on occasion (Luke 24: 25–27) and made passing reference to Old Testament history. He mentioned Moses and the serpent, David eating the shewbread, Solomon " in all his glory," but the long exposition of ancient authorities he left to the scribes. He had all the glorious stories of the Old Testament to call upon, but he borrowed his pictures from the events of daily life: a man sowing a plowed field; a woman sewing a worn garment; a queue of men waiting for a job; a wayside holdup; children playing in the market place.

II. Ethical and Devotional

Preaching on plain ethics has often been under suspicion in evangelical circles. The depreciation appeared to derive from the fact that " it was not the gospel." It was disapproved with a slight pursing of the lips and a disparaging reference to " mere morality." It was supposed that a man whose main staple in preaching was a moral discourse was disloyal in some subtle way to the atonement or the doctrines of grace.

We need not brush this contemptuously aside without a thought on how good men ever came to believe such nonsense. No doubt morals have been preached at times divorced from the gospel and quite neglectful of the word "how." High ethical standards have been reared in the face of defeated men, and no way to the heights has been shown them but toilsome and unaided self-effort. The outcome of such preaching could hardly fail to be depression and further defeat.

Yet the other extreme in preaching is worse and not better. To neglect ethical values and offer instead windy exhortations about "the blood" is not highly devout (as some misguided preachers suppose) but profane and dishonoring to the central sanctities of our faith. In this connection the words of John Wesley, a prince among gospel preachers, might be recalled yet again. He said: "I find more profit in sermons on either good tempers or good works than in what are vulgarly called gospel sermons. That term has now become a mere cant word: I wish none of our society would use it. It has no determinate meaning. Let but a pert, self-sufficient animal, that has neither sense nor grace, bawl out something about Christ, or his blood, or justification by faith, and his hearers cry out, ' What a fine gospel sermon '] " [2]

The doctrinal standards of the Methodist Church are fixed in part by the *Standard Sermons of John Wesley*. Anyone examining those forty-four sermons will be surprised to discover that less than half of them are strictly doctrinal at all, and that a large number must be classified as ethical.

But no one could intelligently dismiss them as "mere

[2] *Works*, Vol. XIII. p. 36. Edition of 1872.

morality." With Wesley, as with all preachers of the first order, faith and works do not fall apart. They preach on faith, and it is not the flatulent repetition of theological phrases; they preach on works, and a man is not left struggling alone.

Ethical preaching is utterly necessary. The gospel authenticates itself at the last in changed lives. The Christian is different in business: his word is his bond. If he wanders from justice, it is only into generosity, never into meanness. He is known as Christ's, not because he says so, but by the way he lives.

Nothing has cast a deeper shadow on religion than the loud-mouthed protestations of devotion to God from people who were known to be risky to trade with, or shabby in private life. When they attempt to silence the preacher's ethical challenge by complaining that he does not preach the " gospel," they have got about as low as they can.

Most people have heard by now of the faithful Negro preacher who dealt plainly with his people about the prevalent sin of chicken-stealing, and other moral weaknesses not uncommon among them. He admitted himself that whenever he preached an ethical sermon " a kind of coldness came over the meeting," and the unacceptable character of his preaching was borne in upon him when the chief lay official of his church told him plainly: " Dis congregation does not like sermons on chicken-stealing, and hopes dat for de future you will keep to de gospel."

It is a dreadful thing when the " gospel " is misused to hide people from themselves, and the need for ethical sermons is by no means confined to the members of one race or of one class.

To ethical sermons, which build up Christian character and aim to depict and destroy our besetting sins, we have linked in this classification sermons of comfort and sheer encouragement, and devotional sermons too.

These devotional sermons are the sermons that carry us farther on the same road. They deal with sanctification. They are calculated most especially for the help of those who are " all out " for the holy life. They are addressed in particular to those who have heard Jesus say, " If thou wouldest be perfect . . ."

The experience of the saints supplies the preacher with material here – this and his own divinely aided efforts toward a holy life. Whatever he has learned from life or from others on how to subdue the flesh, how to quicken the desire to pray, how to deal with oneself in " dry periods," how to " will one will " with Christ, how to forgive serious injuries, how to live in the world yet detached from the world, how to receive the holy sacrament, how really to worship God – all these and a hundred other aspirations of the holy life mark out the wide field in which the preacher moves when devotional sermons are most on his mind.

For the people at the spiritual heart of the Church there are no sermons more eagerly sought or more truly appreciated.

Seldom does an honest preacher preach more to himself. He too would be perfect. God, in his grace, has imputed righteousness to him. God, in his grace, will impart it as well.

III. Doctrinal

For some strange reason doctrinal preaching is always thought to be dull. If one calls it " theological " preaching instead, the expectation is not altered. People seem to shrink from it, and fear that it will not be practical. It was a maxim of the pioneers of Protestant preaching that " doctrines must be preached practically and duties doctrinally."

Their successors must have failed to observe the maxim or people would not dread doctrinal preaching as they do.

Perhaps the name is a little forbidding and people might fear it less if it were made clear that it is simply a *teaching* sermon. The teaching of the Bible on every part of Christian truth has been set out in order and should be easier to understand by its careful arrangement.

Doctrinal preaching is not necessarily " dry." Some men, of course, could make any subject dry! Their capacity in dehydration is unlimited. But doctrine is not dry of itself. If people think it is, let this challenge a man skilled in the craft of sermon construction to prove to his congregation the complete opposite. Let him take the great doctrines of the faith, or aspects of those doctrines, one by one, and show his people their centrality, practicality, and sheer, absorbing interest, until the people hurry to church with the hope in their heart that there will be yet another " teaching " sermon this Sunday morning. It does not require any particular genius to do this. Talent, consecration, and application are enough.

If, contrariwise, a man were to take the view that his people are already well instructed in doctrine, let him test his own confidence by asking a member of his congregation to explain: " How does the cross save? ", or, " Why do you believe in the personality of the Holy Spirit? ", or, " How good can God make you? "

When people talk nonsense about " not wanting theology," or not even " needing " it in religion, they must, of course, be firmly corrected. In a Northern city where I once worked, the local Unitarian minister plastered the walls of the town with a bill saying that he offered " religion without dogma." Standing beside one of his bills, I asked him next day if he believed in God. Friendly fellow though he was, he seemed to resent the question. " Of

course," he said, " I believe in God. You might have known
that I am positive on that."

" Take care," I warned him, smiling. " It is dogma."

So it is! He was not purveying religion without dogma.
He meant " not much of it," and he meant " mine."

But such muddled thinking is no better when we hear
it in Trinitarian churches, as, for instance, when a church
official says: " I don't care for doctrinal preaching. ' Our
Father ' is good enough for me."

What an immense amount of doctrine is hidden in those
two words: the existence of God, his nature, his relations
with men, and the relation of men with one another! When
our hearers tell us that they hope we will not give them
doctrine, we can but repeat the words of our Lord, " Ye
know not what ye ask."

It is, however, one of the encouraging signs of the times
that the keener-minded people in our Protestant churches
are asking for *more* teaching. Neither vague exhortations
to be good nor a running commentary on current affairs,
nor even ethical appeals if they are unrelated to something
larger, are satisfying them now in place of a sermon. They
may not even know the word, but they are feeling the need
of a metaphysic. What is the structure of the universe? To
whom does the world belong? What purpose lies behind it?
What are the Christian affirmations? To what positive
teaching am I committed if, indeed, I have embraced this
faith?

Assailed on one side by a Communist who may be an
atheist also, and, on the other side, by a Roman Catholic
zealot, who certainly knows what he believes and has a
pat answer to everything, many church-attending Protestants have felt the need for clear dogmatic teaching and
are asking their preachers to give it them in a way they
can understand.

We may be glad that it is so. For preacher and people alike, no mental discipline could be better, for soul as well as mind. Without this strong framework of positive teaching, and this firm foundation in dogma, we are, indeed, lost souls on this planet. Nothing else that we say has basis. Our evangelism, our ethics, our social gospel, our sermons on the deep devotional life, all hang in the air.

Some preachers are only exhorters. It is an honorable office, recognized in the New Testament. Yet happy is that congregation whose preacher is a teacher as well.

IV. PHILOSOPHIC AND APOLOGETIC

We have already suggested that to help some people at the point of their need one must start earlier than the Bible starts. A moment's reflection will show that no irreverence lurks in that statement.

Because the Bible everywhere assumes the existence of God and man's moral accountability to him, the Bible is already ahead of many men who wallow in a morass of unbelief. They do not accept the Bible in any sense as the Word of God. Peremptorily to dismiss them because of that unbelief is not Christian. Christ was patient with honest doubt. To cite the Scriptures, therefore, in proof of a point, begs the whole question with them. If one is to speak to their condition, one must deal — without aid from the Bible — with primary questions like this: "Is God there?" "Does God care?" "Can I know him?" "Will he make me sure?"

Anyone who has served on a religious brain trust, where the audience includes non-Christian people, will recall that the emphasis in the questions has a way of falling on these elemental problems. People do not ask if Paul wrote The Epistle to the Hebrews, or whether a Christian may buy ice cream on Sunday. They are down at the rudiments, and some of them are desperate in their longing to know.

The darkness of doubt, especially for those who have once believed, is very terrible. It is true that doubt is sometimes simulated as a screen for moral failure, and it is true also that occasionally young people, who have never really known doubt, pretend to its possession on the supposition that it is intellectually superior to have doubts about Christianity.

But it is not really hard for a skilled counselor to see through these sinful or silly subterfuges.

The real thing is terrible, as anyone knows who has walked that way. What a blow can be dealt to the simple faith of a girl mother who watches her baby die in convulsions! How hard it is for a man still to believe in God's love who watches cancer unhurriedly kill his young wife, and do the work so painfully and so slowly that she is made hideous to look upon before the last stroke is given!

Is God there? Does God care? These are the questions that clamor for answer, and you cannot begin to give the reply by saying, on the authority of the Bible, "God is love." One must begin earlier than the Book itself.

Here, then, is a task for the preacher — a task so old and so hard that he cannot even hope to be completely satisfying.

Yet he can hope to do something. By making himself as much a master of the philosophy of religion as is possible to him, he can confidently promise to cast *some* light on this dark road: he can assert with assurance that the problems are by no means so hopeless as they seemed at first and that, if his Christian explanation is not altogether adequate, no other explanation is worth calling an explanation at all. He will be on his guard against claiming to answer everything. He knows that there are wide margins of mystery in God's dealings with men which the acutest mind and the most reverent heart cannot pierce, but his patience and tenderness and understanding will give hope to the hopeless and some, at least, will venture forth in faith again.

Clearly, this will not be the preaching of every Sunday. A man who made this the main diet of his pulpit would find that there are not so many insoluble problems as all that.

He would find also (and this would be dangerous indeed) that if his pulpit were constantly concerned with problems, he would be putting doubts in the minds of his people that were not previously there.

The passing years make one more able and more skillful in this kind of preaching. To suffer oneself, and to find God in the suffering, is the greatest equipment. You may still lack an answer philosophically adequate, but you have found one that is spiritually satisfying. One's own bitter experience gives authority to the preaching. The people say within themselves, " He has suffered and he knows."

The transition from this type of preaching to apologetics is easy; indeed, it is already made.

There is need for a greater study of Christian apologetics. All preachers who make close contact with the unchurched multitude are struck by the poor caricature of Christianity that people honestly entertain in absurd supposition that this is our faith. Many men imagine that we are defending positions we have long since abandoned — if we ever held them. They are startled often because we have a complete reply to questions they supposed we should find unanswerable. It happens sometimes that they do not ask the questions we should find most difficult, but are held up by perplexities that are no perplexities at all.

Great service can be rendered to unbelievers by this kind of preaching. Great service can be rendered to believers also. A loyal Christian, assailed in his office or work-shop by the taunts or honest objections of people who do not believe, feels more fit for the fight when the answers he needs are given him from the pulpit and he knows the solid grounds on which the faith rests.

If a man feels himself too ill-equipped in philosophy to handle this kind of preaching, he would do well to leave it entirely alone. Raising problems one cannot answer, or to which one cannot make even a seventy per cent reply, is a serious disservice to the cause.

There are many wide fields in which the preacher can still work. Let him cheerfully leave this to other men.

V. Social

More controversy has raged around what is called " the social gospel " than any other section in the classification of the subject matter of sermons. There are those who would make it the whole substance of preaching. There are others who would exclude it from the pulpit alto-gether.

Let us make sure, first of all, what we mean by the term, and then it will not be difficult to see that both extremes in this controversy are wrong.

Two segments of preaching are really covered by this phrase:

First, the fighting of social evils: the campaign of the Christian conscience against those sins that entrench themselves in strong vested interests and batten on the moral degradation of men and women, e.g., intemperance, gambling, slums.

Secondly, the outworking of the Bible doctrine of so-ciety in the community and the world, involving the most complex problems of economics, of sociology, and of inter-national relationships.

Both aspects of the subject bristle with difficulties, though it cannot seriously be doubted that the second are more complex than the first.

But let us recognize, before we proceed farther, how painfully limited is the view of preaching entertained by both extreme schools of thought in this connection: i.e., those who would utterly exclude social preaching from the pulpit and those who would preach nothing else.

The congregation that never hears of the social nature of the gospel will be narrow in its outlook, small in its thinking, and spiritually debilitated. Observe that we have said the social " nature " of the gospel — not the social " aspects " or the social " implications." It is less than the truth to say that the gospel has social " implications." It is social in its nature. That man is purveying skim milk who rigidly confines himself to what he calls the " personal gospel." And it is not even " personal," seeing that " person " implies relationship. It is merely *individual,* and engrossed with man in his separateness.

It is impossible even to hope that this unvaried preaching can ever affect the world in a wide way. It will, of course, affect it for good in *small* ways. Wherever people are held to strict personal standards of truth and honesty and purity, it cannot fail favorably to influence the community in which they live, but it cannot be mighty.

It cannot challenge the organized and powerful forces that engineer large profits out of the frailty or misfortune of men. It cannot bring perceptibly nearer the Reign of God on earth. Indeed, it is not without interest to notice that the exclusive stress on individual preaching belongs to those communions (or those sections of larger communions) that have no expectation that the Reign of God on earth can ever be aided by the effort of men, and who teach a detachment from the world that sometimes in-

cludes abstention even from voting. Apocalyptics they find
more engrossing than the quest for world peace. The im-
minent return of our Lord fills alike their hopes and their
expectation.

But consider the contrary.

Think of a pulpit entirely engrossed with the social nature of the gospel. Imagine a people making their way to
worship and mournfully wondering whether they will
hear of the United Nations, the Iron Curtain, the color
problem, the atomic bomb, racial discrimination in Africa,
racial exclusions from Australia, the evils of the profit system, the rent racket in the slums, the wealth of brewers,
and certain of one thing only, that there will be no personal word in it; no balm for a breaking heart; no strength
in temptation; no sure word about God.

Both these are horrible extremes. Both are wrong. Let
us scrutinize this kind of sermon, quite certain on one
point, namely, that the virtual excommunication of each
of these extremists by the other is patently foolish.

That aspect of social preaching which deals directly
with the social sins is easier to handle. Certainly (and
what a snare this is for the preacher!) it is easier to denounce. Drunkenness, lechery, gambling, warmongering
. . . it is not hard to display a fine frenzy over these human follies and sins. Nobody defends them — or not in that
form! The publican does not like drunkenness. He says
that it "gives the beer a bad name." The "turf account-
ant" protests that he wants his clients to risk only what
they can afford to lose! . . .

No wise preacher spends much time in sheer denunciation. It is not spiritually healthy for people constantly to
hear those sins denounced which they do not commit. It
gives them a false sense of pride and may blind them to
the sins they *do* commit.

Moreover, denunciation of acknowledged sins gets nobody anywhere. The deeper questions concern the cause and the cure. Why do men and women become alcoholics? Was it the desire for fellowship in the first place? Is the Church doing all it can to provide conditions of easy and natural fellowship where strong drink is resolutely barred?

Or why do men gamble? Is it not a natural escape from the monotony of mechanized industry? Is it surprising that the thought of sudden wealth should appeal to people whose interests are limited and whose income, so far as they can see, will always be more limited than their interests? Is there not something ineradicable (and even fine) in the human love of a risk? And, if that is so, how can that instinct be sublimated?

Here is the widest scope for the preacher. Let him live as a pastor, close to his people's needs. Let him get close also to those who never darken the door of a church; to whom, maybe, the rich treasures of art and music and literature have never been opened, and to whom a pint and a pipe and the pools make up the chief interest of living. Preaching with compassion toward this multitude, he will find denunciation cool into understanding, and moral passion translate itself into practical help.

By far the harder part of preaching the social gospel is not directly concerned with social sins or social salvage work. It concerns the immense problems of translating the Christian ethic into the relationships between states and classes, high finance, international banking, and all the matted questions of usury. To talk of it with intelligence and helpfulness requires a knowledge of economics few parsons possess, and a capacity both to read statistics with understanding and to make them live for unlettered men.

It is at this very point that ministers, seized with the importance of the social gospel, and daring on occasion to deal with it in a large way, expose themselves to the most damaging criticism. Some of the criticism may come from those who feel that their own gains may be adversely affected if all preachers take up the same cry, and they protest against such preaching and plead for the "gospel" out of self-interest topped off with a halo.

But the complaints will come also from those who wonder what ordinary people can do about it, even if all the minister says is true, and who regret the use even of occasional sermons for matters that go so completely over their heads.

The preacher living close to God will know what to receive and what to ignore in all this. Always he will be seeking God's plan in the world disorder. He will speak with care, and with becoming reserve, of those things outside the range of his own expert knowledge. He will make clear when it is the Word of the Lord and when he is offering an opinion of his own.

And he will not be fettered too much with the thought that he must have the answer to every question he raises, but count it a not unworthy return for his toil to have posed the right questions and had them considered in the light of the Sermon on the Mount.

Nor will he — even if he carries the specialized scholarship this kind of preaching requires — ever make it the main substance of his ministry. He will recall the hour when, as a youth, Lord Stamp, the eminent economist, was constrained to dedicate his life to Christ at the invitation of an evangelist. Half-baked economics from the pulpit would not have captured that youthful heart, even though Stamp was destined to give no small part of the scanty leisure of his distinguished life to the outworking of the Christian ethic in the economic realm.

In this indirect way, the evangelist may serve the explication of the social gospel beyond even his most ambitious dreams.

But he will not deny as an evangelist the right and the duty of preachers more able with social problems than he is himself to deal directly with economic questions on occasion, and he will bless God for the men who can do it with assured knowledge, penetrating insight, and unmistakable spiritual power.

VI. EVANGELISTIC

Just as some preachers argue with a show of reason that all preaching should be Biblical interpretation, so others contend with similar cogency that all preaching must be evangelistic, i.e., preaching for conversions. Indeed, it is not unknown for controversialists to combine the two and offer the combination as a simple recipe for Christian preaching anywhere.

And in the main, they are right. If Biblical interpretation is allowed to include any preaching that has a sound Biblical basis, and if evangelism is not narrowed to emotional appeals, and no denial lurks in this definition of the legitimacy of doctrinal, philosophic, or social preaching in their clearly defined places, few Protestant preachers will contest the statement that a Biblical basis and an evangelical purpose should characterize the majority of sermons.

Unquestionably, the great end of Christian preaching is to win men and women to a whole-souled committal to Christ and to their spiritual upbuilding in him. Where the evangelical appeal is rarely or never sounded, an awful incompleteness hangs over the whole work.

Indeed, it can be argued that all other kinds of preaching both presuppose and prepare for evangelism. They presuppose it because only a man who had already yielded to the evangel would be deeply interested in Biblical interpretation; in devotional and doctrinal sermons; in the philosophic or social problems that the acceptance of the faith flings up. On the other hand, all other preaching prepares for evangelism by making clear God's will in his Book; showing the solid structure of revealed truth in dogma; clearing away the impediments to faith that any rational man might feel in a world like this; and outlining the way in which God can transform, not only individuals, but communities and nations as well. All this aids evangelism. To the instructed mind, freed from crippling doubt and already catching gleams of the world as God could make it, the evangelist says, " Come! "

But our concern at the moment is with evangelical preaching as such; not with a word of fitting appeal at the end of a flinty piece of philosophic reasoning, but with sermons the whole aim of which is to persuade the will. A sermon such as this might well conclude a series addressed in the main to the mind; this one goes right for the *will*.

There is something stubborn in human nature the moment the central citadel of the will is attacked. It is a deep conviction of the normal man that he belongs to himself. Nothing affronts human nature in the raw more than the assertion, " Ye are not your own." Even when their doubts have been dissolved, and their problems are on the way to solution, and their need of forgiveness all laid bare, there is that in human beings which meets the offer of Christ by saying, " We will not that this man reign over us." That is the keep of the castle which the evangelist must assault at the last, and it calls for all the consecrated cunning that he can command.

Evangelical preaching has fallen under some condemnation in the past because it was said always to assail the will with waves of feeling. Snap decisions were snatched from people emotionally overwrought. The failure of the " converts " (often falsely so called) to go on in the way of life that they had publicly avowed brought this whole approach to preaching into disrepute, and has left in large sections of the Church a positive dread of what is called "emotionalism." In some circles even a warm glow of the most genuine feeling in the pulpit is frowned upon as offensive, and the man guilty of it is in danger of being dubbed " a ranter."

One may hope that that nonsense is passing away. If certain itinerant evangelists in time past were guilty of dreadful sentimental bathos (and they were!), how foolish to suppose, or to wish, that life could be so filleted that all expression of feeling would be firmly cut out. Feeling is, at least, a third of this complex thing we call human personality. To imagine that guilty sinners on their way to the cross must be forbidden all expression of emotion, or that forgiven sinners returning from the cross must be denied a vent to the rapture in their souls, is to ask the impossible and to make nonsense of life in so doing. It leaves one wondering if the people who fear, and forbid it, have ever been forgiven themselves, or known the longing for a thousand tongues to sing the great Redeemer's praise.

The evangelical preacher like a skilled pilot will mark the clear limits of his course and take especial heed where the deep water is. He will know the difference between sentiment and sentimentality as clearly as he knows the difference between sensuousness and sensuality, and he will steer with the calm confidence of those who feel the pressure of God's guiding hand.

He knows that when one has done all the explaining and all the arguing, one has still to do all the persuading. That last stubbornness has still to be overcome. It is not entirely irrational. Man was never made to kneel to his own kind. Only God has the right to put a man on his knees. It should not surprise us that we meet difficulty in bringing sinners there. God, maybe, had greater difficulty in dealing with us.

But, difficult or not difficult, the task is plain. Evangelical preaching is preaching for a verdict. Let the little gnostics and mental know-alls think it naïve if they must. " Come to Jesus," is the plea of the evangelical preacher; " behold, behold the Lamb! "

Our examination of sermons classified according to subject matter is now complete. It is sixfold. There is, I believe, no other category to add. It will be borne in mind that we are dealing at present with the *theory* of preaching. How to approach the practice of it will concern us later. It will be borne in mind also that many sermons — perhaps a majority of them — may include elements of any two or three types that we have distinguished here, but that does not rob the classification of value. The clear recognition of what is a genuine kind of Christian preaching is fundamental to the study of homiletics. The types can blend as they will later. What is important is that we recognize what is truly within the scope of the Christian pulpit, both for itself and as a guide for detecting those spurious forms of preaching that clamor for admittance where they do not belong.

Let us notice, therefore, that nothing is said here about " topical preaching " or " life-situation preaching," both of which receive emphasis in some schools of thought.

The reason for their omission is clear in both cases.

" Topical preaching " is a term variously used. It was employed at one time in contrast to " textual preaching " and to distinguish those sermons that did not expound a text so much as a theme. They usually *began* with a text, but the text was a starting point rather than the whole field of survey. The topic could be (and, a generation ago, usually was) right at the heart of the Christian message: "Doubt: Its Cause and Cure"; "How to Resist Temptation"; "The Ministry of Pain"; "The Atonement of Christ" — yet "topical" was a loose and unhelpful term because (as the instances given show) it made no distinction between a doctrinal sermon, a devotional sermon, and a sermon in apologetics.

In that sense of the word, therefore, the term was not so much false as rough and is, in any case, superseded by the classification we have adopted.

"Topical preaching" in its modern sense is a different, and far more dangerous, thing. It appears to be commoner in North America than in Europe, but it is known in all the continents. It is not preaching, as we understand the term, at all. It is most certainly not "a manifestation of the Incarnate Word from the written Word, by the spoken word." It is usually a moral comment on the events of the day, i.e., the topics of the hour. Whatever chances to be in the public mind and in the press is carried over into the pulpit. "That is what people are thinking about," it is argued, "and we lose no time getting their interest because we have it already."

But people are often thinking about the most shallow things — the luck of a game, the result of a race, the appeal of a film, the shape of a hat. . . . Even if they are thinking about the most profound things, they are often thinking of them in a shallow way, and the preacher may be unable to think much deeper himself. Who but a physicist of the rarest order can intelligently discuss the future uses of atomic power? How many people outside his immediate circle can usefully dilate on the psychology of some foreign minister of state?

The pulpit is degraded by topical preaching of this order. It has ceased to be the throne of the Word of God. What little spiritual value such preaching contains — and much more — could be given in sermons we have classified as ethical or social. But in those categories it would still be preaching about *God* and truly based upon the Bible. The "source book" of this topical preaching is not the Bible, but the newspaper, and the majority of newspapers are themselves in sore need of redemption.

To argue in defense of such preaching that the men who employ it always give "the Christian angle" on the topics they take is no answer at all. They have left the choice of their themes, not to the Holy Spirit, but to the caprice of public taste. What they say could have been as easily said in a leader of the local paper. Indeed, that describes a great deal of this topical preaching — a leader from the press and a few platitudinous maxims added. To say that the people like it is getting lower than ever. The customer may always be right in a shop, but not the worshiper in a Christian church. In Christian preaching one may make topical *references* or take topical *illustrations*. Indeed, one is wise so to do, in order to have the relevance of preaching to life clear and plain. But to call this kind of "topical preaching" a main category in our classification would be a sheer misnomer.

If a study of the true types of Christian preaching did no more than warn us against admitting this charlatan to the Christian pulpit, it would have been time well spent.

"Life-situation preaching" comes into a different category. It has its place in our study — though not here. The phrase has been current for some time, but the clearest plea for it that I know was made by Dr. Fosdick.[3]

[3] "What Is the Matter with Preaching?" *Harper's Magazine*, July, 1928.

Those who plead for life-situation preaching take the view that far too many sermons begin with a text, dawdle with it in Samaria or Jerusalem, and quite often never get the theme related to present-day life at all. The preacher takes a specialized interest in the flavor of a Greek verb, or gives a lengthy historical description of the precise circumstances of the Hebrew prophet he is discussing, but what it all has to do with the farm laborer in the transept or the harassed businessman in the back pew, nobody seems to know. Some worshipers even doubt if the preacher knows himself. He is just "preaching" — filling the twenty-five minutes allotted to the purpose with talk!

One way out of his awful irrelevance, it is suggested, is to get the preacher to face an actual concrete situation in someone's life and give the Christian answer to the dilemma. It is not desired, of course, that he talk *at* a particular person, but that he choose a problem common enough to be of interest even to those who are not actually in it — but who may be in it someday. How does a Christian act in *this* emergency? What does a disciple do *now?*

A bookkeeper in the building business knows that bribes are being given in order to get certain favors, and he is expected to fake the figures and conceal the dirty things that are going on. But he is a Christian — with a wife and three small children. The loss of his job would be serious. What should he do?

A nurse in a hospital in the London area was in charge of a ward of sick little children when an air-raid warning was given. They could not be moved. Terrified as she was herself, she was more anxious to keep terror from them. She lied! She said there was going to be a fireworks display and they would soon hear the bangs. They were not to be afraid. As the bombs fell, the children laughed and clapped their hands. "That was a big one, Nurse," they said, when the building shuddered from its nearest miss. Did the nurse do right? If lying is allowable, how can we know the occasions?

There are parents mourning a darling child and men whose business is failing for all their titanic efforts. A hundred instances could be given and each one of them is the starting point of a sermon. A specific project is plain before the preacher's face. Discuss *that* dilemma. Answer *that* problem. Let preaching *do* something. If life-situation preaching, it is argued, widely replaced the traditional approach to the sermon, there is a reasonable chance that the churches would fill again.

We will discuss life-situation preaching where it belongs, i.e., when we discuss "Beginning the Sermon." It is not a new type of sermon; it is essentially a method of starting. It is vitally important in its place, but it is mistaken to suppose that it adds another category to the classification of sermons considered according to their subject matter. Each of these life-situation sermons (so far as they are real preaching about God and man) could be classified under the categories already made. It is true that they may include elements of two or three types, e.g., ethical, devotional, and social, but the elements are recognizable to a trained mind and the whole value of the method is, first, that it begins where the people in the pews are (in Birmingham or Baltimore; in London or St. Louis), and, secondly, that it has one clear and recognized aim in mind, a plain answer to a real problem.

Its fuller consideration, therefore, its gains and its losses, belong elsewhere.

Only one other question need detain us now. The circling year brings a series of "special occasions" in every church: e.g., Harvest Festival, the Sunday school or Over-

seas Missions anniversary, Hospital and Remembrance
Sunday. How do these fit into our classification of sermons
when the subject matter of the sermons is most in our
mind?

None of them — nor all of them together — constitute
another category in preaching. If a man on Hospital Sunday were led to preach on "The Problem of Pain," his
sermon would be apologetic in type. If he thought it right,
however, to deal with the duty of the community in maintaining the hospitals (the voluntary as against the state
system), the sermon would be social in its character. If he
took one of our Lord's miraculous cures, and raised the
whole question of divine healing, it would blend Biblical
interpretation with doctrine and Christian philosophy.

Special occasions do not create new categories in preaching. If a man so misconceives his high office as to flatter
the mayor (in the presence of God!) for "honoring us"
by coming, or dilates at undue length on the "wonderful
harvest display," or uses more than a moment in appreciat-
ing the children's choir, he is mishandling the "special
occasion." He must not magnify himself, but he must not
fail to magnify his office. His preaching must be "a manifestation of the Incarnate Word from the written Word,
by the spoken word."

While a preacher holds that high conception of his office
in mind, his preaching will never be trifling, never shoddy,
and never mean.

III

Sermons Classified According to Structural Type

WE CONSIDERED in the last chapter the classification of sermons according to their subject matter. We turn now to the classification of sermons according to their structural type.

Every well-made sermon has structure, shape, form. It is possible, of course, to fill twenty minutes or longer with sermonic matter that is without form and yet not entirely void. Sincerity, passion, and the blessing of God can do marvels even with the formless. But how much more powerful it would have been had that sincerity and passion glowed at the heart of a well-constructed sermon, and how certain it is that the blessing of God would have crowned it all!

It is not normally a good thing for the structure of a sermon to obtrude, any more than it is pleasing to meet a man so thin that his bones seem to stick out of his body. But it is important that the structure be there to give unity, balance, and grace to the whole. The *strength* of a sermon is so often in its structure. Lacking that, no fineness of phrasing or facility in illustration can ever make it up.

Everyone gains by sound construction. The preacher himself is mightily helped by it: he knows where he is going all the time he speaks. The trained minds among his hearers are helped too: they delight in the steady and clear progression of thought. The less alert among the congregation are helped also; they do not know how, but they feel within themselves that the message is well wrought.

Some preachers keep always to one kind of structure. Like a suburban builder, they have a plan that is pleasing and they use it over and over again. Who has not traveled through those dreary neighborhoods where every house is an exact replica of the one next door and where there is no scope for variety except in the color of the curtains and the cultivation of the plot?

Nor is this a fault only of mediocre preachers. Some *great* preachers have been slavishly attached to one structure. Dr. W. L. Watkinson and Dr. Alexander Maclaren — to mention only two names — were both held nearly all their days by the " three-decker " construction: introduction; three points; and a conclusion. Robertson Nicoll said in his obituary of Alexander Maclaren that he touched every text " with a silver hammer and it immediately broke up into natural and memorable divisions," [*] but it takes nothing from Maclaren's wide and just fame to declare that the hammer was not always silver. The divisions at times were forced and artificial. Truth does not run all the while in one pattern. The mighty preaching of these men did not turn chiefly on their unvarying structure. The structure tended to monotony. The sermons were gloriously redeemed by their other great gifts. We must speak later of the special appeal of the three-decker construction, but we say at once that while it is impossible, of course, to make the structures of sermons as varied as their contents, the aim should be to make them as varied as we can.

If a man works always on one plan, it is impossible to avoid some monotony in his preaching. His keenest hearers

[*] *Princes of the Church*, p. 249. Hodder & Stoughton, Ltd.

know the building he will rear the moment he announces his text. The content of the sermon may be as fresh as new paint, but it is the same old house again. The man whose architecture is splendidly varied has the people curious before the foundation is in. They hear the text and they ask themselves at once, " How will he build on that? "

It is part of our task now to consider the fine variety of structures that are possible to us and to develop our latent capacities for adding to them. The possibility of adding to the types is open to every serious student of preaching, as it is open to every serious student of architecture also. Respecting the canons of my craft, what new design can I create, apt for its purpose and pleasing to behold? If, as we work deeper into the subject, it seems to beginners to grow unexpectedly technical, that should neither surprise nor displease us. The expert must know some things the inexpert can be happily ignorant about. The doctor of medicine does not talk the technicalities of anatomy when he examines his patient, but he has labored to master his science and could give a high-sounding name to every bone and organ of the body if his patient so desired. His patient does not desire, but no small part of the sick man's confidence derives from the fact that the doctor knows a great deal more about the body than the patient knows himself.

Inevitably, there are some technicalities in our craft. We do not burden our congregations with them in any obvious way, though we serve people the more effectively because we have made this technique the object of our close attention. Nor do we desire to detain in our company in this study the man to whom it all seems much ado about nothing. If he tells us that he has been preaching for forty years and knows nothing about all this, we may be tempted to tell him that we have often suspected as much and wished he had known a little more. For ourselves, we are determined to be workmen who need not to be ashamed.

Whenever a preacher settles with himself to preach upon a certain subject — whether it be the interpretation of a Bible text, the exposition of a doctrine, the unfolding of some aid to the holy life, or the consideration of a social question in the light of Christ — there is almost certainly one structure that would sustain it better than any other.

It *could* be handled several ways. It might be possible to do it *well* in either one of two.

But it is almost certain that one structure could be " just made " to bear that freight.

Some sermon structures seem already wed to the various sections of our subject matter as we set them out: e.g., exposition to Bible interpretation, argument to doctrine, and analogy to sermons on devotion. But there is no exclusiveness about it! The classification of structural types and the classification of subject matter interweave in unexpected ways. A social sermon may call for exposition and an evangelical appeal involve us in high argument!

His theme being fixed, no preacher should approach his early brooding on the subject, or his later-heaped-up material, with his mind already committed to one mold. Such an approach cannot fail to damage his work. Being free with many molds, he needs to approach his material with a mind truly open, and invite the bubbling matter itself to select the mold it really needs. Having crystallized his object in the sermon in one pregnant phrase, and having said within himself, " This will I do," let him draw near and question the heart of it with such thoughts as the following clearly in mind: " How can this best be done? Shall I argue the case — a strip of logic as true as steel? Would it be best to make it all explanation — a piece of patient teaching? Shall I keep returning to the central theme, hanging the one truth in varied lights? Shall I cast it all into one large picture? " The skilled craftsman has many, many ways of imparting the truth. His aim at this point of his preparation is to fix the ideal method for that precise need.

No one who has given any serious study to the craft of preaching can doubt that this variety in structural types is of immense importance. It is one of the deeper ways of keeping dullness out of the pulpit. It brings the keenest minds in the congregation to church on Sunday, not only reverently eager for the Word of God, but with an edge on their appetite. It helps to make preaching *interesting* — which it ought to be — and it puts a kind of expectation in people which gives the preacher a splendid start. He looks his congregation in the face and they seem to say, in confident anticipation, "What have you got for us today? " The preacher remembers that it is by the labor and gifts of his people that he is separated to holy things. How just, therefore, that they should come expecting to receive, and how natural also that they should hope that his word will be not only edifying but interesting as well!

In my college days I recall a fellow student returning from the conduct of evening worship in a suburban church and announcing that he had had a wonderful time in preaching. He mentioned the text and said that the structure of the sermon was simple but impressive. He had shown what this particular truth meant:

a. To the individual.
b. To society.
c. To the wide world.

We caught a glimpse of his mind, and a picture of the widening circle of his thought, and dismissed the matter from our conversation.

The following Sunday he was out again, took another

text, and had another wonderful time. The structure, it seemed, was the same again. With this fresh text, he had shown what the truth meant:

a. To the individual.
b. To society.
c. To the wide world.

At the third and fourth repetition, it occurred to us that this was becoming the pattern of all his preaching. "Why not?" he asked. "Anything you want to say can be said this way. It is both personal and social. It begins with a man and it encompasses the globe."

So he went on!

In fairness, I think I should state that he sometimes stood his structure on its head and in order to finish with the personal note rendered the sermon thus:

a. The wide world.
b. Society.
c. The individual.

I suppose one could get by even with this if one preached almost always to different congregations, but imagine the utter boredom of people regularly enduring that banal repetition!

We may be thankful that reiteration is seldom so crude as that, but the extreme case points the moral. We must have variety in structures. That we may have variety, let us study the different types. Our aim now is to classify sermons, not by their subject matter, but by their central architecture.

We may distinguish, I think, five main divisions:

I. Exposition.
II. Argument.
III. Faceting.
IV. Categorizing.
V. Analogy.

We may notice again here (as when we classified sermons according to their subject matter) that the groups have no sharp edges, and are not completely exclusive. Argument may have its part in a sermon the main structure of which is clearly categorizing, and analogy may have a minor role in a sermon carefully cut by faceting.

Our immediate business is to understand what we mean by these five main divisions and into what subdivisions they break up as well.

Let us look at each of them in turn.

I. Exposition

The word " exposition " in connection with sermons has been used in various ways. At one time it was reserved for those occasions when a preacher did not confine himself to a short text, but commented upon a lengthier passage. This was called " expository " preaching, in contrast to " textual " preaching.

The word, however, was not well used that way. Exposition merely means " setting forth " or " explaining," and if a man is explaining a short text, a whole chapter, or a whole book, it is still exposition. His depth, of course, must decrease with the area he determines to dig, but his sermon does not cease to be exposition.

We shall use the word here, therefore, for all those sermons whose direct aim is explanation (and particularly the explanation of the Bible), and, as the mental approach does not vary with the area covered, so neither will our word.

Let us begin with the exposition of a text.

1. *Single text*

There are four common ways in which a text is used in preaching. It can be:

a. The whole area of the sermon.

b. A genuine starting point for a subject it raises.

c. A "motto" — with a discernible relation to what is said.

d. A point of complete departure and used only out of habit.

The last use is a misuse of Scripture. From mere custom men sometimes announce a text which has no relation to their theme at all, and it would be better, in those unusual circumstances, to announce the theme and go ahead. The second use is fully legitimate, and a case can be made out for the third, but when we talk of " the exposition of a text " the first use fills our mind.

Here is the aim: to explain in the simplest words what the text *means*. Every scrap of Greek or Hebrew a man has gathered is now in fee. He will never parade his scholarship (God forbid!), but it will all be at his people's service. If he is unfamiliar with the original tongues, he will not be utterly cast down by that. He will know how precious is an intimate knowledge of the English Bible, and he will compare passage with passage, and so study the context of his selected word that when his sermon is over he can honestly feel that, to the extent of his ability, he has made his people understand the truth of that text. He will, indeed, endeavor to deal with it as a man eats a boiled egg. He aims to empty it of its goodness, though with this significant difference: he can soon scrape the inside of an eggshell to the bottom. To the bottom of a deep text he seems never to come.

Word by word, seeking the overtones and the undertones where they are significant, he will lay the meaning bare. It is the pure exposition of the Scriptures. Done well, it is perhaps the greatest service a preacher can render his people.

2. *Multiple texts*

The work of expounding the Scriptures is often aided by the laying of texts side by side.

a. They can ask and answer questions, e.g.:
  (1) "What is man, that thou art mindful of him?" Ps. 8:4.
  (2) "The Spirit himself beareth witness with our spirit, that we are children of God." Rom. 8:16.

b. They can be used to bring out a contrast, e.g.:

  The Bible knows two ways in which you can be dead without being buried:

  (1) "Dead with Christ from . . . the world." Col. 2:20 (K.J.V.).
  (2) "Dead through your trespasses and sins." Eph. 2:1.

c. They can indicate a distress and describe the deliverance:
  (1) "Upon the earth distress of nations, in perplexity." Luke 21:25.
  (2) "My peace I give unto you. . . . Let not your heart be troubled." John 14:27.

d. They can compel one to see several aspects of a truth, e.g.:
  (1) "Each man shall bear his own burden." Gal. 6:5.
  (2) "Bear ye one another's burdens." Gal. 6:2.
  (3) "Cast thy burden upon the Lord." Ps. 55:22.

e. They can vividly portray a progress of thought, e.g., four judgments on Jesus:
  (1) "He hath a demon, and is mad." John 10:20.
  (2) "He is a good man." John 7:12.
  (3) "Thou art the Christ." Matt. 16:16.
  (4) "My Lord and my God." John 20:28.

The intelligent relating of one part of Scripture to another is mentally fascinating for the preacher and spiritually enriching to his people. The astonishing number of these illuminating combinations in the Scriptures will surprise anyone who has not made a practice of making them.

And it is still *exposition:* i.e., the making plain of meaning, and making it all the plainer because it is another part of Scripture which is called in to help.

3. *Broken texts*

It sometimes happens that the truth of a text is best seen by looking at it in section. Just as a forester can tell some things about a tree only by cutting it and counting the annual rings, and just as a geologist must chip the rock and an architect look at his drawings in section, so must a preacher sometimes snap his text across his knee, as it were, and invite his people to look at the raw edge. It must be done, of course, with skill. It is not hard to imagine into what blasphemy people might slip by undertaking this without reverent judgment, but done well it can open up the Scriptures in unexpected ways. For example:

a. The origin of moral obligation:

" Beloved, if God so loved us, we ought." I John 4:11.

b. Faithful though the flames prevail:

" Our God whom we serve is able to deliver us from the burning fiery furnace . . . but if not . . ." Dan. 3:17, 18.

c. The way of achievement:

" As many as received him, to them gave he power to become . . ." John 1:12.

Observe that it is still exposition. We have simply adopted an unusual device to get an important meaning out.

4. *A passage*

Expounding the Scriptures with full effectiveness is not possible if we always keep to short texts. It is like trying to see a great picture one square inch at a time. Step back! Take a look at times at the whole, and then a more intent look at certain parts.

Expounding a passage is taking a more intent look at certain parts. It guards one against neglecting the context — always a peril when one is expounding a short text — and enables both preacher and people to feel the sweep of the author's thought. The danger at which we have already glanced, of treating a text as a point of *departure,* is quite impossible with this kind of preaching — and a healthy discipline, therefore, for any man whose unhappy bias it is to ride away readily from the Word.

The depth the preacher can reach when expounding a passage necessarily depends on the length of the passage. Inevitably, the wider the area, the more shallow the digging. Clearly, one's *purpose* must determine the amount to be covered. Beneath the overarching aim to nourish the people spiritually is the immediate purpose to do something for them on this specific occasion. The immediate purpose will determine whether six or a dozen verses shall constitute the area of discourse. It must be enough to achieve the purpose — and no more.

Because — this must ever be borne in mind — there are especial dangers in this type of preaching. It lends itself readily to an unready man. Scamped preparation lies behind the utter boredom that expounding a passage often creates. Finding Sunday almost upon him and no solid preparation for the pulpit already made, a man may fly incontinently to this form of exposition, which becomes, in such circumstances, a weak and running commentary on all that is already obvious in the passage he selects to abuse. When "persecuted" in one verse, he flies to the next! Like certain Biblical commentaries, he avoids with unfailing skill every real difficulty that turns up. He says what the Bible says all over again, seemingly unaware that he is utterly incapable of saying it better. He has none of those penetrating insights given to the man who has long brooded over the passage in prayer, nor can he search the inner meaning of the words with the arc light of God.

A generation ago it was not unusual for minor comedians to lampoon this kind of preaching. Avoiding, with a proper reverence, any reference to the Bible, they would take their "passage" from history, or folklore, or a nursery rhyme, but imitate with no little skill the unctuous manner and sententious verbosity of the unprepared preacher.

I remember hearing one of them "expound" old Mother Hubbard. Bits of his droll mimicry float to me down the years:

"Mother Hubbard, you see, was old; there being no mention of others, we may presume she was alone; a widow — a friendless, old, solitary widow. Yet, did she despair? Did she sit down and weep, or read a novel, or wring her hands? No! *She went to the cupboard.* And here observe that she *went* to the cupboard. She did not hop, or skip, or run, or jump, or use any other peripatetic artifice; she solely and merely *went* to the cupboard. . . .

"And why did she go to the cupboard? Was it to bring forth golden goblets, or glittering, precious stones, or costly apparel, or feasts, or any other attributes of wealth? *It was to get her poor dog a bone!* Not only was the widow poor, but her dog, the sole prop of her age, was poor too."

There is enough truth in this foolery to make any serious craftsman solemnly resolve that when, in preaching, he sets out to expound a passage, he will do it with such complete preparation that not even the echo of these caricatures will sound in his people's ears.

5. A book

It is not uncommon advice from people who set out to make the Bible more interesting to their fellows to advise them to read a whole book of the Bible at a sitting. Too much Bible study, they feel, has been "bitty." An apprehension of the real meaning of the Scriptures requires that one occasionally ascend above a whole book in a plane or a balloon and see it all at once from above.

Let the preacher take his people up in a plane. There is no need, on these occasions, that he confuse a pulpit and a professorial chair, and subject his people to a lecture rather than a sermon. Some history, no doubt, will be called for in order that he may panel the book into the contemporary scene, but all this can be done clearly yet with economy in time. As a herald of God, his real business is with the message of God. Let him steer the plane, therefore, that his hearers may see in outline, but in wholeness, the meaning of the Almighty in this piece of canonical writing; let him leave them hugging the warm thought to their hearts that they now understand Hosea or Jonah, James or Jude, and then let him venture on to the harder and longer books as their eagerness for more gives him encouragement. Such a preliminary sermon should always precede any detailed exposition of a book. To attempt to teach the physical geography of a country without putting a map before the pupils would be foolish. It is not less foolish in a preacher. The expositor of the Word must know both how to draw and how to display a large map.

6. *A biography*

I suggested just now that it was a common refuge of the unprepared preacher to " expound a passage " and to bring by his trite prosiness a sound sermonic method into disrepute. A second refuge for the unprepared is a Biblical biography. It seems so easy to " get together." A concordance and a Bible dictionary soon shovel all the known facts into a heap. Setting them in order and drawing certain " lessons " is not heavy labor. The people like the method because, in studying an actual man's life, they feel near to life, and it is one of the widespread convictions of common people that the pulpit and real life seem far apart.

The misuse of the method must not blind us to its high and legitimate place in structural types. It is a true method. It is classified best under exposition because it aims to make clear what is recorded in Scripture. Done well, it is preaching of a very high order indeed.

The Bible was written long ago. All of it has an Eastern setting. It is not hard for those who read as they run to feel that much of it is folklore and to reverence it rather out of duty than out of awesome belief. Those preachers who can make the Bible characters step out of the hallowed page as men of red blood and women of subtle seductiveness, and can make one feel that one would know Delilah and Daniel, Barnabas and Paul, if one met them in a restaurant or a committee, will make the Bible at the same time an enthralling book to all who hear them. Living men and women re-create their era. The timelessness of the Bible comes out in this way. The preacher is analyzing Gehazi but — if only he knew it! — he is analyzing me.

Like all other sermon types, this has its dangers even beyond the illusion that it is easy. Men often construct these sermons more out of their imagination than out of the Holy Book. A most important place for the precious gift of imagination must be left in all preaching, but here, more than anywhere else, it tends to run riot. Preachers start a series on the Minor Prophets, or the apostles, or the kings of Judah, and after a good time with the outstanding characters they find the material for the rest woefully thin. It is just not there!

But the series — like the play — must go on. What the Scriptures do not supply, they "cook up" from tradition or their own speculation. The sermon becomes interlarded with phrases like this: "It has been suggested"; "One eminent scholar believes"; "Is it beyond reason to suppose."

Out of such preaching all authority has gone. The man is a romancer where it is blasphemous to be such: at the throne of the Word of God.

Nor is this — serious as it is — the worst snare of this type of preaching.

The itch to say something new (that fearful plague of preachers) is especially prevalent in these paths. A man forgets that his higher, harder task is to make truisms significant and proclaim an *old* gospel with compelling freshness. The foolish longing to be "original" trips him up and he sets out with dubious evidence to reverse the Bible judgment on many of its major characters. Esau was quite a gentleman. Moses was a bad-tempered fellow. Judas Iscariot meant no harm.

So it goes on! The preacher thinks himself original, though his little heresies have become so common that even that dubious pleasure is snatched from him.

And, all the while, an awful price is being paid for his

vanity. He is unconsciously undermining his people's habit of reading the Bible. It does not mean what it says. If you are specially trained like the minister to understand its deeper meaning, it always seems to mean something else, something opposite. Their lack of expert knowledge frets them. They lay the book aside. The man who should have used his expert knowledge to make them more eager for mining in God's Word has filled them with a crippling inferiority and blinded them to the fact that, for the simple as well as for the profound,

> "The Spirit breathes upon the Word,
> And brings the truth to sight."

One of the keenest Bible expositors I ever knew unconsciously killed the habit of Bible-reading in his church. A really able Greek scholar himself (and no mean Hebraist), his regular method in preaching was to take a text loosely translated in the English version and explain what it *really* means. Month after month this went on: "It *says* this; it *means* that." The people gave up reading the Book. Can you wonder? Within their modest minds they said, "It takes a specialized training to understand the Bible, and a specialized training that we do not possess." So the genuine learning which should have made the Scriptures more inviting was unconsciously turned to this alien use.

Twisting the Bible's judgments on its own characters in the interest of a little originality is another way of doing the same thing. Let it alone! Our business is to expound the Word in such a way that reverence will be heightened and appetite made more sharp. The Bible biography is a true type of sermon. Imagination may play upon the facts, but imagination must not distort them.

7. *A picture*

We live in a picture age. Television and movies are most popular forms of entertainment. Illustrated magazines reach phenomenal circulations. Visual aid has become the handmaiden of education. By the skillful use of word pictures, the preacher can bring himself into legitimate harmony with common taste.

The transition from Bible biographies to picture sermons is easy to see. There is, in fact, an intermediate type — part picture and part biography: e.g., Moses before Pharaoh and Moses in the Wilderness; Peter in the Gospels and Peter in The Acts. But these are not picture sermons in the plainest sense.

Any sermon in its illustrations may carry minor pictures, but there is a specific type of sermon that can be called a picture sermon as a whole. It belongs (as its major classification) to exposition, because the pictures are normally lifted reverently from the Bible and the aim of the sermon is to make the picture still more living by revealing comment. Sermons devoted entirely to the exposition of a parable, or the vivid recovery of a single Bible incident, would all come under this head.

Read Alexander Whyte describing the man who knocked at midnight and asked for three loaves.[5] It is not, in its wholeness, a picture sermon, but it begins that way. You *see* the man. You see him wait between his knocks. You see him turn to go home . . . and then turn back again. You hear the dogs bark at this midnight hammering. You see him put his ear to the door and then his eye to the hole. Read it slowly once, and the man who knocked at midnight will be forever real to you. The picture drawn by our Lord in two or three deft strokes has been filled out

[5] *Lord, Teach Us to Pray*, p. 169.

for you, pulled into clear focus, and cast on a white screen.
You have only to shut your eyes and you can see the man
at will.

Preaching can do that. Masterly preaching! Here is no
banal repetition in halting, colorless words of what the
Bible has already better said. This is the thing alive. What
our Lord said in the condensed speech of four verses is
shown to us in honest detail. No violence is done to the
original. No time is lost over vain reiteration. It is just
held up for all to see, and ever afterward a light shines
from that picture on the problem of importunate prayer.
One may still lack a complete solution. One may still ask
mistakenly why we must persist in pleading with a loving
Father for what is so plainly right, but the light from the
picture is enough to walk by. You can see the man leaving
his friend's house with all his thanks spilling over and his
arms happily encumbered, not just with three loaves, but
with as many as he needs!

Much prayer and much brooding and much disciplined
imagination are called for in preparing these sermons. The
man who thinks that it is "an easy option" had better
think again.

So we come to the end of the sermons we have classified
under exposition: sermons whose whole aim (even though
the method varies) is to explain meaning. We may admit
as we leave them that they do not call for the same con-
structive skill that other architectural types require. The
explanation of word and clause is usually fixed by their
order in the text or passage under examination. Yet, as we
have seen, these sermons involve other skills, and it is
arrant folly to suppose that this kind of preaching is "per-
fectly simple" and calls for little preparation. A counter-
feit of these methods *is* simple. A man with a ready tongue

can do it with no preparation at all. But it is dishonoring to the Bible and poor food for those folk who come. The direct explanation of the Word of God requires, as it deserves, the best we have.

We turn next to the sermons that argue a case.

II. ARGUMENT

The sermons classified under this heading are those that lay down a thesis and spend themselves in proving it. Normally, they will be based upon a text, but they are not mainly expository because the whole meaning of the text may not be under review. The subject is announced, if not in the first breath, certainly in the first minute or two, and the sermon marches forward to establish the truth already announced. There should be progression of a kind in all preaching, but in this kind of preaching it should be plain before the people's face. We are moving to that end. Here and there on the road, no doubt, we shall be impeded as I throw up, in all honesty, an objection to my line of thought, but, as that is rebutted, we shall move on again. Here is a direct appeal to your God-given faculty of reason. Are you not compelled by the very logic of things to believe the truth of this? So believing, are you not compelled also to act in this way?

There are, however, various ways of arguing a case, and we may subdivide them in the manner of formal logic into deduction and induction. The difference between the two, for those who have had no training in logic, may be roughly expressed as the difference between analysis and synthesis. The two approaches are not opposed. Indeed, they belong together. It is the starting point that is different.

When we look at a system of reality, we may look at a number of propositions expressing relations that hold universally within the system — the fruit of men's past questions and successful answers. Or, contrariwise, we may look at reality in its particulars, which are awaiting explanation through the universals they express, but universals which, at present, are not fully understood.

Now when we begin with the established universal (e.g., All men have sinned) and bring a particular person, because of his humanity, under that universal condemnation (even though he protests, in the way of modern man, that he "never did anybody any harm"), we are working deductively.

When, on the other hand, we consider such a question as whether the use of all the means of grace is necessary for the holy life, and heap the evidence together that every saint of whom we had knowledge prayed and studied the sacred writings, we are working inductively to see if we can establish a universal. We shall be forced in such an inquiry to consider the sanctity of hermits, who cut themselves off from all Christian fellowship, and the Quaker saints, who never partook of the Lord's Supper, but the difference in our approach to the problem is clear.

Both methods, if properly used, are valid. As all logicians agree, they are complementary.

1. Deductive

There is a "tightness" and satisfaction in deductive argument not, in the nature of things, possible as yet in induction. The universal principle is established — at least in the evangelical world: "All men need a Saviour. All men can have a Saviour. All saved men must witness to their salvation. All saved men must press on to holiness."

_____

[6] The following few pages may seem slightly technical to the reader unfamiliar with logic, and the scope of this book does not permit a fuller discussion. An elementary course in the science of reasoning is of incalculable value to a preacher.

Many of these "established universals" of evangelical preaching can be set down and form the major premises of powerful arguments and appeals.

The syllogism lies behind most of this arguing. A syllogism is an inference from two propositions that contain a common element. One of these propositions, at least, must be a universal. Put together in the right way, a new proposition can be reached that is more than the sum of the other two, but whose truth is a necessary consequence of theirs.

Put at its very simplest, a great deal of evangelical preaching might be expressed like this:

> All men need a Saviour.
> You are a man,
> Therefore, you need a Saviour.

The simplicity of the illustration will not blind us to the importance of the structure. From facts already accepted in the mind, we want to draw other facts not so readily accepted, and we want to press them home with such conviction that they will carry conviction to all who hear.

But an argued sermon will seldom be so simple as that — or so bare. Quite often one must fight, first, for the acceptance of the universal in the unregenerate minds of men. Normally, the preacher must raise (as the only speaker) objections to his own arguments, if he is shrewdly aware that those objections are already in his hearers' minds. If the argument is to carry, it must carry *them*. One cannot stand and utter it to one's own satisfaction alone. Hence the halts to pick up this party, or to fight off that opposition, so that at the last the preacher reaches home, not alone or with the gullible handful, but with a compact host who have been constrained to believe.

Sometimes an argued sermon is best begun with a dilemma. A dilemma (if the technical terms may be forgiven) is a syllogism with a compound hypothetical premise for the major, and a disjunctive proposition for the minor.

An illustration will put it plainly.

Many a Christian man of sensitive conscience in England found himself wrestling with a problem like this during the war:

"If I serve as a soldier, I shall be expected to kill, and that is against my conscience.

"If I do not serve as a soldier, merchant seamen will still perish bringing food to me in our island home, and that troubles my conscience.

"But I must either serve as a soldier or not serve. Therefore, however I act, I must have a troubled conscience."

In handling a dilemma (which can, of course, be both simple and complex) one can attack the premises or deny the legitimacy of the inference, or talk of other possibilities, but to see a congregation perk up at the announcement of a dilemma that is close to their daily life is very stimulating to a preacher, and, as no sensible man would propound the dilemma had he not something helpful to say in its solution, he can strike ahead exhilarated by the keen expectancy of his people.

Nor do the forms of deductive reasoning end even here.

An able, argued sermon can have a sorites at its spine. A sorites is a progressive line of argument simplified in expression by the omission of the conclusion of each of the prosyllogisms.

A simple illustration of the Aristotelian sorites might be expressed thus:

All good fathers seek their children's good.

All who seek such good have true regard for God, the source of good.

All true regard for God implies honoring and worshiping him.

All honoring and worshiping of God sets a good example.

Therefore all good fathers set a good example.

A preacher need not be familiar with the technical terms of logic and may seldom (if ever) use them in the pulpit, but the discipline of logic will do him incalculable good. Exercise in the clear definition of terms, studies in classification, the development of a keen scent for fallacies, marking the limits of legitimate inference — all these are of unspeakable help to a preacher. If the opportunity to study formal logic passes him by, let him at least scrutinize, in the light of God, the chain of reasoning in every sermon that argues a case. Let it be, to the limit of his ability, *honest* arguing. A very proper reverence for God's house secures the preacher from interruption when he is preaching, but let no man presume on the dumbness of the congregation to press upon them unconvincing arguments that would not constrain a schoolboy. Howsoever the argument is clothed and illustrated and pressed, let it be as sound as one can make it, and if, as sometimes happens, there is a weak link in the chain, admit as much. You gain more than you give away. It registers on the mind of every intelligent hearer that you are a mentally honest man.

2. *Inductive*

We have already made clear the nature of inductive reasoning. It builds up from particulars. It depends on observation, testimony, the framing of hypotheses and their final establishment. It is a fascinating sphere for a preacher. Done with respect to the rules that govern sound induction, it can delight the preacher in its preparation and bless the people in its delivery.

Imagine a man preparing a Sunday morning sermon that aims at deepening the devotional life of his people. Almost inevitably he will find himself dealing with some aspect of prayer. But not the problems of prayer this time. This sermon is directly to feed their souls rather than to clear their minds, so it cannot be on this occasion, say, " The Pain of Unanswered Prayer."

No, but it could be — yes, it *could* be, " The Pain of *Answered* Prayer "!

Ah! What about that? It is not always bliss to have your prayers answered. When you ask God for guidance, you sometimes hear things you would rather not hear.

Is that experience known in the Scriptures?

Yes! Isaiah knew it. He prayed for light and trembled when it came.[7] Have I known that experience myself? Have I seen it in others?

What about the saints? Do they mention it? Augustine does most certainly. He says so in the *Confessions*. Take his testimony. He is a dependable witness. What of Saint Francis? and John Wesley? — why, yes, and David Livingstone too? Heap their experience together. Can we now venture on the hypothesis that it is a dangerous thing to ask God for light: dangerous to comfort, to worldly security, even to ecclesiastical preferment?

But, just a moment! Is there anything on the other side? It is, of course, the wisest thing in the world to pray for light. All real progress is progress in God's light. This must be balanced . . . but I see the way! " The Pain of Answered Prayer " is the subject: Isa. 21:4 is the text. I can tell a chorus of testimonies from the saints and I can cite also my own soiled heart.

So the sermon begins to take shape. It is devotional in its

---

[7] Isa. 21:4.

subject matter, and yet it will argue a case. It shows once
again how subject matter and structural types interweave
in unexpected ways. It builds up, as all true induction
must, from observation and testimony to hypothesis — and
the hypothesis, as the preacher hopes, will have its final
" establishment " in the hearts of his people.

Some of the most powerful sermons that argue a case
argue in reverse. They might be called " demolition " sermons. Instead of setting out to prove the truth of some
great Christian doctrine or principle, they set out to dis-
prove some widely accepted generalization of secular life;
e.g.: " Try everything once "; " When in Rome, do as Rome
does "; " It will all be the same one hundred years from
now "; or some article of unbelief more strongly en-
trenched than any of these.

The structure of the sermon is not materially different,
except that one is knocking down instead of building up.
The demolition sermon can be deductive or inductive in
approach. But let the arguments march. Keep only to the
strong points. Throw away minor things in your favor lest,
in dwelling on them, you create the impression that your
case cannot be overstrong if you need *that* to support it —
for people will answer that minor objection in their own
minds and deceive themselves that they have answered
the whole case.

Nor — and this is especially important — should you be
so crushing that you create sympathy for an opponent so
completely routed. Let there be no pride in the perform-
ance. Expose the false thing with all the power you possess,
but not with such self-conscious cleverness that you create
an impression of contempt for the foe. Not even sin is con-
temptible. Always in contempt there is some admixture of
pride. It is to be doubted, therefore, if it should ever have
place in the heart of a Christian. In the pulpit, most cer-

tainly, it should find no room.

One danger of all sermons that argue a case is that they may become heavy. Too much logic can weary people. A man who leaves the impression that he is more interested in his subject than in its object is failing. To help the people is the aim even more than the logical completeness of the argument. One hopes that the two can go together, but if it ever becomes a choice between them, the help of the people takes precedence.

But the two things need not fall apart. Let a man take extra care with his illustrations when the main structure of his sermon is closely reasoned and logically tight. Let him take care also to repeat with pleasant variableness the progress of the argument up to each point he has reached. Let him be careful also for the *order* of his arguments, beginning with something already accepted by the people so that all start together, and mounting to arguments of more serious import and of greater force as he moves up to the climax which he hopes will move their wills.

To throw in at the end a few weaker arguments as a kind of " makeweight " has the precisely opposite effect to the one he desires. Do not throw them in: throw them away. From that last, strongest, most appealing point of all, let him move in a stride to his triumphant " Therefore. . . ."

And with God be the rest!

III. FACETING

I have borrowed this word from the lapidary. An uncut gem can look very rough. Only an expert would know it for what it is. One can see in a shop window in Regent Street, London, exact replicas of all the great diamonds of the world before they were cut, but they look like dull, misshapen lumps of glass.

The experts knew them for what they were. Split and cut, they have become the treasure of kings.

Cutting a precious stone after it has been split is a skillful task. It is called "faceting," i.e., cutting faces on it that its beauty may be better seen. It is the simple truth to say that apart from this highly skilled work the depth and the sparkle and the translucent loveliness of the stones would never have appeared.

That is at least partly true of the truth of God. It may be that the fault lies with our eyes, dazzled by the glare of this world rather than with the precious stones themselves, but, whatever the reason, the preacher's task is to make the truth beautiful by his craftsmanship, and one form of the craft I call "faceting." It is cutting "faces" on a gem of truth to release both its whiteness and its gleaming wonder.

When a lapidary cuts a stone, he always cuts to a pattern. It needs hardly to be said that he does not take the stone rough and cut three or four facets unrelated to one another. There is a design in his mind. The cutting itself is a work of art. The light that shoots out from the several faces when his work is done dazzles and delights the eye of all who really look.

The preacher must cut to a pattern. There must be a relation of harmony between the various "faces" on his gem of truth. It does not matter for the moment whether he is cutting direct upon a text, or cutting on a theme he has announced. It must have a pattern: some indication must be shown *why* he was cutting when he cut that way.

It is to that form of sermonic style that we now turn. It is not direct exposition, seeking the meaning of each word and clause of the text. It is not a progressive argument, a case to be established by the sheer force of logic.

It is holding up one gem of truth on which the preacher has cut certain patterned facets and turning the truth in the white light of God.

Let me show what I mean by half a dozen instances. They are by no means exhaustive. An hour of thought would produce as many more. The pattern for the cutting is in the title and in the clause that follows it.

Faceting may proceed:

1. *By origins* (" The cause of this is . . . ; " e.g.:)

   Why have we lost the men from the churches? Five thousand turned out to hear Jesus (John 6:10).

   a. There is a fault in our presentation of the message.
   b. There is a fault in us as messengers.
   c. There is a fault in the men.

2. *By consequences* (" The fruit of this is . . . ; " e.g.:)

   What comes of neglected devotions?

   a. Loss of inward peace.
   b. Loss of assurance.
   c. Loss of power in witnessing.
   d. Loss of sensitivity to God's guidance.

3. *By implications* (" This requires that . . . ; " e.g.:)

   " Thou shalt love thy neighbor *as thyself.*" Mark 12:31.

   a. We recognize the legitimacy of self-love.
   b. We seek our own good *in* the whole.
   c. We watch with wakefulness our awful bias to self.

4. *By concrete instances* (" This is shown by . . . ; " e.g.:)

   An abstract truth made vivid by clear instances: " The righteous shall live by faith." Rom. 1:17.

    a. From Scripture.
    b. From history.
    c. From modern biography.

5. *By eliminating false likenesses* ("This isn't that . . . or that . . . ;" e.g.:)

There is an inevitable conspicuousness about the Christian. Christ "could not be hid," Mark 7:24. But Christian conspicuousness is not *fame*.

    a. Fame is a thing people aim for.
    b. Fame can attach to anything.
    c. Fame is often freakish and sudden.
    d. Fame is ephemeral.
    e. Fame brings burdens.
    f. Fame has bitter disappointments.

6. *By the means to an end* ("This is the way to . . . ;" e.g.:)

    a. Acquire a certain virtue.
    b. Conquer a certain vice.

It has been well said that the neglected word in preaching is the word "how." So many sermons, excellent as a delineation of a certain virtue or excellent in their exposure of a certain vice, leave off too soon. They never get to "how." It isn't hard to make the members of a Christian congregation long for a lovely virtue as one limns it in a saint. It is not hard to make them hate a dirty sin as a man, from personal and bitter failure, can so describe it that they feel it stir in their own stained hearts. But how? That is what they want to know. Are there no "techniques" to share? — no down-to-earth explanations of the way good men and women acquired that grace or sloughed off that sin?

How?

Under this heading, therefore, I include all "How to . . ." sermons; for example: "How to Offer a Personal Witness for Christ." "How to Deepen the Desire to Pray." "How to Receive the Holy Spirit."

Every ethical and devotional sermon requires the "how" in it. But it is good at times to make a whole sermon on the "how." I classify such messages under this section of faceting and give them a high place among the sermons that greatly help.

It may be asked whether any rules can be given for the craft of faceting. I think, perhaps, that a few can usefully be given.

Keep the pattern clearly in mind all the time. "I am cutting to *that*" — origins, consequences, implications — whatever it may be. Cut to the one pattern, therefore, throughout the whole sermon.

Do not cut one face upon another. It is not unusual to notice in immature preachers that, of their three or four divisions, two may be subdivisions of another, and material gets muddled between them. The pattern is not being kept in mind.

Although this kind of preaching is not a progressive argument, all preaching should advance. It should be moving up all the time. Study a well-cut gem. Usually, there is a fine central facet, around which the smaller ones are gracefully arranged. Move up to that central, shining, lustrous face. Let the light gleam from that at the last. Hold that finest, most moving truth before them as you close. As with a precious stone, the central light seems to gather all the others into itself. If, moreover, that last point carries a particular duty for them as individuals, that will be better than a general truth which leaves them without obligation to go away and do something.

Some men seek to make their sermon divisions (howsoever they fix them) alliterative or chiming. There is no harm in this just so long as they are exactly representative of the meaning, but straining for either is repugnant and seems to treat the congregation as a collection of juveniles. We cannot always have our headings " Pardon, Peace, and Purity " or " Get, Forget, and Regret," to take two examples I heard recently. That device, when it is laboriously engineered, had best be left to the leader of the junior department of the Sunday school, in whose work the practice has some justification.

IV. CATEGORIZING

We turn now to a form of sermon structure that bears certain superficial similarities to faceting, but is quite clearly distinguishable.

The method breaks up the material of the sermon into various categories. The categories imply and complete each other. In faceting, so long as the harmony is maintained and the truth is being imparted, there is no necessary limit to the number of " faces " that can be cut. In categorizing there is normally a recognized limit. Fixing one determines the others. The pattern, therefore, is plainer, with both the gains and losses that that implies.

The method can be best seen in examples, though, again, the instances I give are not exhaustive and are, in these first illustrations, deliberately simple and bare. The categories may be drawn direct from the text or, if the subject of the sermon is announced in a phrase of one's own, from the theme itself.

Categorizing may proceed, therefore:

1. *Under the person to whom the appeal is addressed or to whom it has reference,* e.g.:

   a. An evangelical appeal

      (1) To youth.
      (2) To the middle-aged.
      (3) To the old.

   b. A devotional sermon: Love in relation to

      (1) God.
      (2) My neighbor.
      (3) Myself.

   c. A social sermon: How will this affect:

      (1) The working classes?
      (2) The middle classes?
      (3) The upper classes?

   d. A missionary sermon: Can this be presented to:

      (1) Believers in the ancient faiths?
      (2) Primitive people?
      (3) Westerners who have lost their religion?

2. *Under enlarging areas of application,* e.g.:

   And here we might classify the structure beloved of my friend of college days! What reference has this truth to:

      (1) The individual?
      (2) Society?
      (3) The wide world?

3. *Under different elements in personality,* e.g.:

   The artifices of sin:

      (1) Thought — which it wickedly confuses.
      (2) Feeling — which it dangerously inflames.
      (3) Will — which it perilously ensnares.

One does not need to be a pulpit genius to see the living flesh that could clothe so bare a skeleton with vigorous life. Let a man consult his own heart concerning the genesis of sin in him, and let him trace also, in some hour of burning self-revelation, the way in which smoldering desire smoothly rationalized its way into his thought and finally pushed him over the edge. Biography rushes forward with other illustrations, but self-knowledge is a preacher's clearest guide. As he traces the dirty thought through the tunnels of his mind, his hearers will look at him in fearful wonder because he is telling them " all that ever they did," and he himself will be tempted to break a chief rule of public speech and utter his thoughts, not looking the people in the face, but half shamefully looking down at his own boots.

Or one might approach the different elements in personality in a sermon calculated to *deepen the longing for holiness* which lies somewhere in the heart of all men. How is this to be done? To what parts of a man's nature can the appeal be addressed? To:

(1) Ambition: Directed aright, this is a good thing. " Ye, therefore, shall be perfect . . ."

(2) Reason: My mind tells me I was made for goodness: this is the way to integration.

(3) Conscience: The sense of "ought" within me points inexorably up.

Or the spiritual mastery of life may be inculcated by a sermon proving that *Christianity does not fillet our personalities,* but takes the raw material of human instinct and touches it redemptively. There are three chief driving forces in this nature of ours, and with Christ in control they have dignity, beauty, and delight:

(1) Self. I matter. I was dear enough to shed the precious blood.

(2) Sex. I am not completely creaturely. I am cocreator with God.

(3) The herd. I belong to others by His ordaining. They need me and I need them.

Anatomy is not beautiful except to the rare enthusiast. When the bones of the little princes were discovered in the Tower of London, they were just bones. They would not have suggested to the uninstructed mind the comely boys to whom they belonged.

Nor does a sermon skeleton suggest very much to those uninstructed in our craft. It is just bones. But *we* know their importance, and even the person least interested in the technique of our task would admit that there are important differences between a baby and a jellyfish.

4. *Under varying periods in time*

Time is one of the major categories of all philosophic thought, but, in the sense in which we are employing the word here, we may subdivide time into the simple categories of common life (past, present, future), and we may divide the past into a hundred different "periods" according to our knowledge of historical research and according also to our historical viewpoint, e.g.,

> "Thou hast beset me behind and before,
> And laid thy hand upon me."
>
> Ps. 139:5.

Here is an instance where the categories are actually offered in the text:

(1) Behind: All my yesterdays are covered. He saves me from my soiled past.

(2) Before: All my tomorrows are anticipated. He is undertaking for my future.

(3) Just here: In this very present He lays his hand upon me.

One can turn into a new year with a singing heart if one has a tonic word like that.

Or one may take a sweep of history and give some solid teaching on the nature of the Church by a sermon on apostolical succession as understood by evangelicals. Some Christians, stemming down in unbroken succession from the undivided Church, see the Church as a divine society visibly existing on earth and secured in its purity by " one blest chain of loving rite." Others see it as called into being on the initiation of the Word of God and the response of faith, and it is focused for them in the doctrine of justification *sola fide, sola gratia.*

This second conception of the Church might be set out in a sermon entitled "Apostolical Succession as Understood by Evangelicals ":

(1) The Word in Paul.
(2) The Word in Augustine.
(3) The Word in Luther.
(4) The Word in Wesley.

The way these great figures call to one another across the centuries can all be set out — and not least that moment about " a quarter to nine of the clock " on May 24, 1738, when, at the reading of Luther's Preface to Paul's Epistle to the Romans, the apostolical succession in this deep sense was passed on to John Wesley.

Or — jettisoning the controversy latent in this — one may take the same outline to show the spread of the Evangel through the ages, and make it either one sermon, in which it would remain "outline" even in delivery, or a series, in which each era could be treated with some fullness.

Categorizing in periods of time is almost limitless, though a man whose special interest is in history would need to watch his enthusiasm (as other men must watch theirs) lest it become a structural form from which he seldom breaks away.

5. *Under different ways in which a situation can be met*

Almost any conceivable situation in which mortals are called upon to act presents them with a number of choices — though, usually, a limited number. The clear presentation of the situation, and an examination in turn of the variant ways in which one might respond, can lead forcefully to a plea for the Christian way as the best of all.

The world outlook may be dark. Indeed, no one may know how to act and say, incontrovertibly, *this* is the Christian way.

Yet there is still a Christian *attitude*. We can face even our perplexities in a Christian or sub-Christian or unchristian way. We can:

(1) Give it up. Despair of the future. "Eat, drink, be merry."

(2) Carry on. It is grim and practically hopeless, but let us keep our human dignity.

(3) Embrace the future. God is on the throne. All will ultimately be well.

Or we may take a similar illustration from the Children of Israel at the Red Sea, Ex., ch. 14:

(1) The people said, "Go back."

(2) Moses said, "Stand still."

(3) God said, "Go forward."

We are not here concerned with the flesh and blood of these sermons. That later! It is the *form* of them that matters to us now. We have admitted that a sermon can be without form and — such is the grace of God — not utterly void.

But it borders on the miraculous. No sermon is really strong that is not strong in structure too.

V. Analogy

We come, finally, to the sermon structure that is all analogy. It is not a form to use frequently, though it has the highest sanction in the practice of our Lord, and may be studied at its best in him. He said: " I am the vine "; " I am the door "; " I am the way." Modern sermons can be built on this pattern, and when this is done skillfully and freshly they can be most effective: e.g.: " Life as a Voyage "; " Life as a Cricket Match "; " The Devil as a Bowler "; " The Christian Life as a Military Campaign "; " The Church as an Organism " — twenty examples leap to mind at once.

But it is a method easily overused. The analogy often gets pressed too far. Enthusiasts with this structure sometimes run down to details, and may even run down to absurdities. It is not always simple to know where to draw the line. Paul likens the Church to a body, and mentions the eye and the hand and the foot. Did the preacher overdo it who, handling the same analogy, told some members of his congregation, not that they were an eye or a hand or a foot, but that they were the tonsils ("We are no worse off when you are gone"), and the appendix ("We did not know we had you till you caused us trouble"), and the artificial teeth ("Sometimes you are in and sometimes you are out")?

But there are graver dangers even than this roguish

"improvement" on Paul. The method can become juvenile. It can be a mosaic of fairly obvious and even trite comparisons strung together with the repetitive phrase, "And we may liken this to that."

Analogical preaching is a genuine type of structure and carries the highest authority. It should receive infrequent use and most especial care.

And here we conclude our examination of the main structural types. Let it be said again that it should be every preacher's aim to add to the structures just so long as they are sound and strong enough to bear the weight he wants to place upon them. Let it also be borne in mind that, in delineating the main structures, we do not contend that they have always or usually to be kept "pure." We found in our classification according to subject matter that an actual sermon might include elements from two or three sections: e.g., Biblical, ethical, and evangelistic; or doctrinal, philosophic, and evangelistic. We found, also, in relating subject matter to structural types, that while, say, exposition belongs most naturally to Biblical interpretation and argument to apologetics, the structures and the subject matter may interlace into scores of varieties. It is important to notice now that these main structural types we have distinguished *combine among themselves*. Argument is called for, at times, in exposition. An analogy may serve to bring out the brilliance of one surface of a sermon cut by faceting. If someone, the better to understand what we mean, were to ask us to characterize one of our Lord's sermons, for instance, and chose "The Sower," we would answer at once that He was categorizing *within* an analogy. The mail structure is clearly analogical: human hearts likened to soil. But within the analogy he categorizes the various kinds of soil: the soil trodden hard by wayfarers, the thin skin of soil on rock, the thorn-choked soil, and the good earth. The combination is plain. It is not less plain that the range of combinations is almost infinite. We have admitted that we cannot hope to have our bone structures as varied as the flesh with which we shall clothe them or the features that they will finally wear, but let no man conclude that the range of structures is small.

Only one other question need detain us now. We made reference in the early part of this chapter to the three-decker construction and have said nothing about it since. And yet a surprising number of our illustrative examples expressed themselves in three headings. Is this coincidence — or does it belong in any way to the nature of thought?

Some people think that there is a deep explanation. It may be an echo of syllogistic reasoning, which requires, as we know, a major premise, a minor premise, and a conclusion — although the three heads of sermons often have no other likeness to a syllogism than this coincidence of number. The reason may lie even nearer the heart of philosophic thought, which proceeds, as some believe, by thesis, antithesis, and synthesis. The explanation may, indeed, transcend all terrestrial things and relate itself to the Holy Trinity in most mysterious ways, and reappear in all creation as creative idea, creative energy, and creative power.[8]

But, on the other hand, it may have an explanation far less sublime than these. Two points in a sermon leave many men with insufficient material; six points overload the people's mind. There is a certain " naturalness," maybe, in a threefold division and the prevalence of the custom must have some explanation more than custom itself.

Yet, having conceded so much, it cannot be too emphati-

[8] Cf. Sayers, *The Mind of the Maker*, p. 28. Methuen (Harcourt, Brace & Company, 1942).

cally asserted that the slavish breaking up of the material into three, when nothing in the material itself requires it, is stilted, wooden, and tends to monotony. The three-decker construction is really a misnomer in homiletics. It is not a true structural type. The threefold division may appear, and appear with power, in all our main structures, but it is not a structure as such. Unless exposition requires it, or argument, or unless you choose to facet with three faces, or categorize under three heads, it has no claim *of itself* to be imposed upon material, and the blind following of the practice is to be deprecated — even when it is the work of distinguished men.

If, in an expository sermon on the parable of the Prodigal Son, you chose to trace the mind and movements of the boy thus:

(1) Sick of home.
(2) Homesick.
(3) Home,

it will do, and it will help because it is fair to the story and may make your development and amplification of the theme a little more manageable.

If, with a social subject in mind, you want to categorize the various attitudes of people to the world, you might set them down like this:

(1) Those who *abuse* it: the flagrant sinners of all kinds.
(2) Those who *refuse* it: enclosed nuns, monks, and Protestants also, afflicted with the wrong kind of otherworldliness.
(3) Those who *use* it: all who accept God's will in it and employ it as a vale of soul making.

In both cases, the threefold division is natural, adequate, and serviceable, but the material invited the divisions. The divisions were not imposed on the material.

So great a preacher as F. W. Robertson made only the slightest use of three headings. Indeed, his own danger was to work always with two headings and to become confined within that mold.

Be confined in no mold. See the wide variety spread out before you. Observe again the possibilities of combination. Come to truth with such freshness and with such mastery of structure that no one, hearing you announce your text, will be able to say with confidence, " I know how he will treat that."

IV

Sermons Classified According to Psychological Method

WE HAVE classified sermons according to their subject matter.

We have classified sermons according to their structural type.

There is still a third way in which we may, and must, classify them. We must classify them according to their psychological method, i.e., the way in which the preacher plants his message deep in his hearers' minds by studying their minds.

When the subject matter of the sermon is clearly determined and the preacher's object in his message plain before his eyes; when the structural type, or combination of types, has been definitely fixed because that one is clearly the best means of conveying the truth, there still remains this other question: What is to be the mental and emotional relationship between the preacher and people? How are the little tendrils of personality which reach out from one to another to touch, engage, and hold firm?

Some people would brush such questions impatiently aside. They might even tell us that they have been delivering powerful sermons for years and never thought of such a thing. In their opinion, a man makes up his mind what he wants to say, stands up with a modest bearing, and gets it said as clearly as he can. Having said it, he sits down. That is all there is to it. Discussion about psychological method seems to them a darkening of counsel with words.

There is more in it than that. Even the man most scornful of talk about psychological method is aware, if he is a powerful preacher, that there is a moment when he makes real contact with his congregation, and a moment later when he takes tight hold of them, and a climactic moment when he can do with them almost anything he likes. He may never have analyzed in his own mind how he does it. The Spirit of God working upon a gift of God in nature may enable him to do it without ever considering the " how " of it at all, but he would be foolish to assume that there is nothing to study and nothing to learn.

There is a psychology in actual preaching quite apart from the preparation to preach. Why do some men " grip " and others fail to grip? The answer to that question may be difficult, but the person who just patters about " magnetic personality " is not even trying to answer it. Moreover, the man with the gift may not himself be aware how he uses it, but none of these objections debars us from attempting to understand it ourselves. An aura of mystery, no doubt, will hang about it at the last, but it will be no small help if we can begin to understand the answer and make some elements in it altogether plain.

The progress of a sermon may be measured two ways: mentally and emotionally. One can test it by the unfolding of the thought; one can test it by the mounting tide of feeling. Some sermons, it is true, make a far lower bid for feeling than others, but no real preaching excludes it. Not even the profoundest philosophers achieve " pure thought," and our congregations are never composed entirely of philosophers. Moreover, a " manifestation of the Incarnate

Word" cannot be given without feeling — feeling in the
herald and feeling in the hearers. The progress of the sermon, therefore, can be measured in either of those ways:
How does the thought march? How does the feeling
mount? Clearly, the two should be related. A bad order in
the importance of the argument will create chaos in the
rhythm of the feeling. Many a prentice preacher must have
wondered, after a good start to his sermon, why the thing
began to sag and the people to fidget uncomfortably in
the pews. Were the people to blame — or he himself? Having got their attention, how ever did he come to lose it?
Ought he to be able to say to the people in his heart, " Give
me your attention for five minutes and take it away afterward if you can "? Then what happened today?

Maybe he has forgotten that if you start on the top rung
you cannot go any higher and that all your " progress "
must be downward. The reaction in the feelings of the
people was entirely normal. They were going down with
him, but they reached the bottom before he reached the
end.

The relation between the mental and emotional progress
of the sermon may be tested in another way. People whose
main interest in life is in ideas, and who go only occasionally to public worship, sometimes complain at the slow
progress in the unfolding of a preacher's thought. To them
the preacher seems to hang on to an idea overlong. He
may, in fact, keep returning to the same idea down different avenues of thought, and hanging, as it were, a
single truth in varied lights. " I've got that," they say to
him in their minds. " I got that five minutes ago. So what?
Get on! "

Theological students often react in similar ways. All
their time is being given to ideas, and religious ones at
that. They want the thoughts of the sermon to march, not

like infantrymen, but like riflemen.[9] It must be a quickstep
to suit them. They have no wide experience of handling a
large and varied congregation. They do not understand,
as yet, the psychology of the mixed crowd. When the
argument hangs awhile, time is not being lost. If an ex-
perienced craftsman is at work, it is instructive to observe
what he is doing. He is resting the congregation, perhaps,
after that harder bit of thinking. He is repeating the point
in a fresh way for the sake of the slower members of the
flock. He is picking the gallery up and piquing the interest
of those whose minds are distracted by the cares of the
week. He is keeping the mental and emotional progress
parallel. He will not move to the next point until they have
glowed over this one, and, when they do move, he will
see that they feel the exhilaration of going up.

" Progress " in the sermon, as this master craftsman understands it, is not just progress in the unfolding of his
ideas to his satisfaction, or even the satisfaction of the
intellectuals and pseudo intellectuals in his congregation:
it is the progress of as large a body of the people as he can
get to move at all, and at as swift a pace as is possible with
so heterogeneous a crowd. That requires the skillful blend-
ing of idea and feeling. He is driving two horses. It is no
small part of his skill to see that they keep together.

It belongs also to the craft of psychological méthod to
see that the progress of the sermon is pointed by subclimaxes as it moves on to the supreme climax of all. In
those sermons that rigidly argue a case, it is sometimes
hard to secure the subclimax. Everything awaits the final
" therefore." The logic may get heavy. The reasoning may
be so close-knit that stragglers begin to fall away from the
main column within five minutes of being on the march.

---

[9] The famous Rifle Regiments of the British Army march farther
than the normal infantry — 140 to the minute instead of 110.

It takes no little craft to keep them together. One must rest awhile here on an illustration and smile together, maybe, over some whimsical absurdity that comes to light; but the measured rest is soon over, and we are off again.

The subclimaxes are easier in categorizing because every category has a climax of its own. The subclimaxes are easier still in faceting because every facet has a glory of its own. Indeed, in faceting one can often parcel out the conclusion of the sermon by minor " applications " as one completes each " face " of the truth, though moving all the while to the largest facet of all and gathering the minor applications together at the last.

Climbing Snowdon by some of the routes is not climbing up all the time. There are minor peaks on the way with splendid views. There are strips of the path where you run down a little before the steep ascent begins again, and more than once you feel, " This is the top," and then discover the serene peak beckoning you up again. The intermediate " summits " are lovely and rewarding and well worth a rest awhile. But, Y-Wyddfa outtops them all. This is the supreme summit. Now you can survey all Snowdonia. It was worth every step to see this.

So with the well-wrought sermon! There are minor peaks as we move on to the greatest peak of all: moments of thrill and vision, but, all the while, the inviting prospect of more and better to come. So preacher and people mount the slope together, refreshed by the intermediate vistas, but eager for the sovereign vision which shall crown it all.

Four main psychological methods may be distinguished:

       I. Authoritative.
      II. Persuasive.
    III. Co-operative.
    IV. Subversive.

We shall notice here, as in the previous classifications, that the sections are not rigidly exclusive. A sermon may easily include elements of two or three. We shall notice, also, that just as one structural type attached itself most naturally to one section of the subject matter (e.g., exposition to Biblical interpretation, and argument to apologetics), so one of these psychological methods will attach itself more naturally to one of the structural types (e.g., authoritative to exposition, and persuasive to argument). But, again, there will be no exclusiveness about it. It adds to the infinite variety of sermons that these methods interweave, and a message broken up by categorizing can be an adventure in co-operative thinking, and an argument against the faith can be skillfully undermined by a subversive attack.

Let us look at each of the methods in turn. Their combination and unusual use must all wait upon an understanding of what they are in themselves.

I. AUTHORITATIVE

The expositor of the written Word must be a teacher. The man whose task it is to explain the doctrines of the Church must be an educationist. Inevitably, therefore, when the preacher comes of set purpose to make authoritative meaning clear, his method must be didactic.

The odor of the schoolroom — which some people find slightly unpleasant — hangs around this word, but the line the preacher must take can be made clear if we mark the dangers of too much pedagogy — and too little.

The preacher *must* have authority. Is he not the herald of a Great King? Is not the awesome conviction in his mind, " God has sent me "? Do not the faithful members of the flock, convinced that God calls men to be preachers of his Word, carry in their minds also the acknowledgment, "God has sent him"? Is it not clear, therefore, that authority must mark the preacher of the Word?

But it is not an authority that the man has to assert in words himself. The authority is in his office and in his work. Because it is the Word of God he is expounding, it must have weight, and power, and sway. He does not vend the Word: he proclaims it. He does not hawk it: he announces it. He does not timidly proffer the divine message: he placards it in the face of all men.

Few things are more sad to observe in the pulpit than a man half apologetic for his gospel, who hesitatingly brings something out of the treasury of God in the manner of one saying, "You don't want this, I suppose?" Imagine a teacher addressing her youthful pupils on the multiplication tables and saying: "Would you mind believing this? I should be so much obliged."

There are times when the note of authority is called for, and it is called for supremely in the proclamation of the Word of God. Proclaim it, therefore! Tell it out! "Thus saith the Lord." There is that in man which inwardly craves the note of authority. He might resent it from another man, but he concedes its fittingness if it comes from God. If that is the Word of God, let me know. Do not offer it "upon approval" because my wayward heart will never approve. Face me with it! Compel my attention! Give me no peace until I find peace in Him!

But notice this! Because that awful authority belongs to the preacher's office, he must be forever on his guard against the sinful supposition that the authority belongs to himself. The most grievous consequences can follow from this confusion. If it be a pitiful thing to see a man in the pulpit half apologizing for his gospel, it is a worse thing to see a man appropriating the authority that belongs to him as a representative and attaching it to his own unimportant opinions. Something quite offensive obtrudes into his manner then. " I'm telling you," he seems to say, and the " I " looms uncommonly large. He seems to thrust himself forward in a way that creates revulsion in the mind of many people and his hearers adopt a mental attitude of opposition. " I don't care if he is right," they feel. " I won't take it from him."

The distinction between the herald proclaiming his King's message and the braggart proclaiming his own message cannot really be confused. The man knows the difference in himself and the hearers know the difference also. In the one case there is no self-assertion: the man is clearly humble and not a little bewildered that God should use him as a mouthpiece. His authority is clearly derived. He speaks out with awful boldness, but somehow he does not fill the picture. It is easy to forget him altogether and find yourself dealing with God alone.

In the other case, it seems all self-assertion. Pomposity clothes the preacher. He is aware of his gifts and " I can do this " is the overtone of so much that he says. The people turn from him, not because they resent the authority of God's messenger, but because they resent the assumption of authority by the messenger himself.

From the shoals of timidity and diffidence on the one hand, and the rocks of egotism on the other, the preacher will carefully keep away, most especially when his message in preaching calls for the authoritative method. He is plainly teaching with the highest warrant. This is the word of God through his Book. This is the word of God through his Church. The preacher is laying it down in no uncertain way, but he is only the herald. " Take no notice of me," his whole manner clearly says, " but, as you value your soul, take heed to my words, for this is the message of the Great King."

II. Persuasive

But the preacher is not always a simple expositor. There are times, as we have seen, when he argues a case. The congregation is now, not a set of pupils in a classroom, but one huge jury. He means to get the right verdict from them all.

There is no concealment of his purpose. Just as the jury in a court of law know quite well who is the counsel for the prosecution and who for the defense, so with this psychological method in preaching. The aim is announced. Quite early in the sermon the preacher makes it clear what it is that he is going to show or prove, and what course of action he is eager that his hearers shall adopt.

The old question discussed among preachers as to whether or not it is best to announce one's divisions beforehand is all answered in this study of psychological method. In persuasion — yes! One may leave out the announcement of the intermediate steps until one comes to them in order to have the element of surprise in reserve, but there can be no surprise about the major aim. In this method, that must be clear from the start. All the power of the preacher in memory, mind, and will is bent to persuade; all the resources of heaven he calls to his aid that the will of his hearers may resolutely move in the right way.

Yet it is possible to convince a man's mind and not constrain his will. One's logic may be mentally irresistible and yet a danger to one's cause. The defenses that the hard-pressed soul puts up may be read from his mind like an open book, spoken aloud, and then smashed before his face. At the last, he knows he is mentally beaten, and yet he will not give in. The will, "the keep of the castle," as we called it in Chapter II, has not surrendered. All the outer battlements are taken, but he will not haul the flag down.

Every able preacher bears that final obduracy in his thought. Somehow, he must convince the mind and not antagonize the will. He must not allow his hearers to retain a whole heart in opposition. He must get within the defenses of the keep. Logic cannot do this. Love is the only artifice here — the supernatural love that God gave him for the souls of men when he made him a preacher: the love that surges in his heart at worship when he faces his people and feels as though his arms could shoot out and embrace them all.

Never does the preacher's love for the souls of men have freer play than when he deliberately sets out to persuade. The naked heart of God which he has seen displayed in the cross is all before him now. God loved as much as that. He died in agony for these men and women. The angels in heaven wait to rejoice over one sinner that repents. One must repent tonight. " God give me one! At least one! "

So he bends himself to his task: exposes the weak excuses of sin in the minds of his hearers, yet does it with such tenderness that he never antagonizes them but seems to say all the time, " I have been guilty of such folly myself." So he goes on until his voice seems their *own* voice, the voice of a long-dead self, but a self strangely rising into new life. They stir into soliloquy. " No longer is the preacher speaking outside me or against me. It is my best self he is pleading and all the accusations are in my conscience now. My heart is capitulating almost before my mind. I *want* to be convinced. Preacher, *I'm on your side!* Bid me come. The voice of God is in your voice. Bid me come and not all the powers of hell shall hold me back."

This is the place where " the wooing note " comes into preaching. It is not so much a matter of choosing words,

still less is it a matter of elocution. It is the longing for
souls planted in a man's heart by the Holy Spirit and kept
intense by much secret prayer. It *will* out! Every guilty
sinner knows it. " This man cares for me. He is pleading
like a father with his wayward son. I will arise and go to
my Father."

It needs hardly to be said that evangelical preaching
calls for this method of approach. It demands persuasion
— but so also do social and apologetic preaching in their
somewhat different way. Among the structural types it
is intimately related to argument, but almost every type
invites it when the closing moments come.

III. Co-operative

It troubles some preachers that the pulpit is separated
from the pews and lifted high above them. They feel that
it creates a gulf between themselves and the people. The
actual physical gulf seems to suggest to the people, they
fear, that there is a mental and spiritual gulf as well. How
to get on the same level as the people is their aim: How
to make it clear that preachers are men of like passions
and perplexities with the troubled souls within the pews.

The psychological approach to preaching that we have
called " co-operative " is one way of overcoming this difficulty. It is best explained, perhaps, in the mental attitude
that the preacher adopts. He is not now the preacher as
teacher. He is not now the preacher as advocate. He is
now the preacher as perplexed man.

The sermon often begins with a puzzling text, or a problem of life, or a difficulty of belief, or a seemingly insoluble
social question. In any case, it brings a pucker to the brow.
The preacher does not start like a teacher with the answer
all prepared, and an answer which is to be taken on authority. He does not begin like a partisan, saying in effect,

" This is my view and I want you to share it also." He begins just with the pucker. "Phew!" he says, "what do we make of this?" and he begins by putting himself mentally alongside the people, apparently as dismayed as they are by the problem which is raised.

He sets it out, first, by simple thesis and antithesis in order to make the perplexing difficulty of it still plainer to any who has not felt it already. For a few minutes it gets darker than it was before.

Keeping to the collective "we," he begins to lead them in the search for an answer. He makes it, by his manner, a common quest. "We can start here. We all agree about this." He moves on to a clearer path by apparently casual phrases like: "Do you suppose . . . ?" "Of course, we might consider . . ." Presently, the quest warms up! Clearly, we are on the scent of something good. It is not so perplexing as it seemed. It is, in fact, positively illuminating. The keenness of the people increases as the unraveling goes on. The pace quickens. A little breathless, maybe, but wonderfully exhilarated by the search, preacher and people burst together on the complete solution and share the delight in finding what they had so arduously sought.

If there is a danger in the authoritative method of appearing to talk down to the people, if there is a danger in the persuasive method arising from the fact that one so obviously holds a brief, both are guarded against here. The quest of truth is made a common task of preacher and people. When the congregation see that pucker on their minister's face, they know within themselves that he needs their help in solving the problem (!), and the effort has almost the excitement for them of a detective story.

The method has dangers, of course. It requires the highest degree of preparation. A man must know with precision where he is going. The uncertainty is only in the phrasing. The "discoveries" must be clear, definite, recognizable, and, in their cumulative effect, fully satisfying. If a man gets lost in the maze himself, or gives the impression after the first few minutes of not knowing where to turn, he will achieve the precisely opposite effect from the one which he desires. He may even leave his people wondering why he chose a subject he could not handle, and raised perplexities he could not solve.

But, done well, it is fine preaching. Never do pulpit and pew seem nearer together, nor a congregation so much in its minister's heart and hand.

IV. SUBVERSIVE

This is a method to be used sparingly and only after men have had a great deal of experience in preaching. Even then it requires an unusual congregation if it is to achieve its full effectiveness.

Put quite simply, the method is this. The preacher assumes an intellectual position that he does not really hold, but that he has the best cause for knowing is held by other people; e.g.: that the Bible is not a dependable guide to conduct; that the fear of the Lord has nothing to do with wisdom; that teetotalers are a lot of silly cranks; that bookmakers are benefactors of society.

Placing himself in the position of people who hold one of these views, he begins ostensibly to argue for it. He gathers together the poor reasons that support that opinion, and one by one he tries to make the most of them. After each point, and almost as an aside, he is obliged as an honest man to make certain damaging admissions against the point already made. The admission invariably makes the previous point nonsensical, but he "labors on" until the sheer absurdity of the thing topples over in his hearers'

minds and the case he had apparentlv embraced collapses
by his own skillful undermining.

As the method may be a little obscure without illustration, let me give a hint or two of how it works.

Imagine a man setting out to prove that the promoters
of football pools are public-spirited gentlemen whose
whole concern is to help the country by providing the
people with a harmless occupation on winter evenings,
and whose deep desire, even at a loss to themselves, is " to
scatter plenty o'er a smiling land."

One could begin with a cut at those spoilsports who
object to people's spending two or three evenings a week
working out their permutations (though it must be reluc-
tantly admitted that they could greatly widen their education and usefulness if those three evenings were spent
in another way).

One could point to the people who have won reasonably
sized prizes in this great agency of human good will
(though it is not to be denied that they are only two per
cent of the whole).

It should not be overlooked that the generous promoters
of these golden schemes offer a fortune for so small a sum
as a penny (though a silly fellow interested in math has
worked it out that the chance of forecasting fourteen correct results in the penny points' pool is 4,782,969 to one).

Nor should it be forgotten that these largehearted mil-
lionaires are providing work for thousands of people
(though somebody at the Ministry of Labor takes the view
that the 80,000 clerks employed in the 300 pool factories
might all be doing something useful for the nation in its
time of economic need).

It is a lying insinuation to suggest that the pool promoters are gamblers (because, of course, their profits are
sure: whoever wins or loses they always win: their " rake-

off " is a first charge on the sixty million pounds a year
that change hands in this way).

Nor can the Government grumble. Do not the people
who support the pools send 8,000,000 to 9,000,000 letters
a week and keep the post office busy supplying the postal
orders? (though there are foolish fellows who actually believe that the post office could be better employed and
the sixty million used for cancer research).

Enough has been said to show how the method works.
Its dangers are quite patent.

In a general congregation, a slow-witted person might
actually suppose that you were supporting the practice
you pretended to embrace, and either take up the habit
you were undermining or lose faith in your soundness of
moral judgment. It is possible to be too smart. Daniel
Defoe found that. In the days when " Dissenters " were
persecuted in England, and their rigid exclusion from all
forms of public office was warmly advocated, Defoe wrote
a pamphlet, *The Shortest Way with the Dissenters*. It
advocated, not repressing the Dissenters, but exterminat-
ing them altogether. Defoe hoped, by the help of irony, to
laugh the persecutors out of court. Unhappily, he had the
misfortune to be taken seriously and to hear his work
lauded from the pulpit. Samuel Butler met with a similar
experience when he published *The Fair Haven*. Irony
requires a select audience.

The subversive method must be used, therefore, with
restraint, and one must be sure of the mental quickness of
the whole congregation. I have found it effective with congregations in college chapels. Chapel was not compulsory,
perhaps, but some constraint had been put upon the men
to come. Not a few came unwillingly and prided themselves on being unorthodox. Their attention could be arrested by a preacher who seemed as unorthodox as them-

selves. Once caught, it was not hard to hold their interest. The artifice of it was clear to them in five minutes but, in this unusual way, the truth was punched home.

So we conclude our classification of sermons according to psychological method. Let it be said again that the same sermon may include more than one approach. The authoritative and the persuasive can so easily blend. The subversive or the co-operative may both of them provide the method of one section of a sermon whose main approach really belongs elsewhere.

Combinations may come as they will. Our immediate aim has been to see the methods " pure."

It should now be possible for us to put almost any sermon upon the dissecting table and dismember it. We should be able to tell its blend in subject matter, its general architecture, and its psychological approach. The constant reading of other people's sermons is not to be commended to preachers, but the occasional dissection of a published sermon is most excellent practice.

Do not be depressed if, as a beginner, you do not find it easy to classify the parts. The anatomy of sermons is by no means so simple or constant as that of the human frame.

But it is rewarding.

Put a sermon by a master on your table. Question it. What was he after? How did he go for it? By what means did he secure his effects? How strong is its central structure?

With the threefold classification in mind, you have the instrument that will dismember every part.

V

The Beginning of the Sermon

IT IS impossible to exaggerate the importance of the beginning of the sermon. Most of our hearers give us their attention at the start. However convinced they may be that preaching is boring, hope springs eternal and the thought lingers in the mind of the most blasé that perhaps on *this* occasion something of the awful majesty and arresting power they would associate with a message from God may be evident in what the preacher has to say. If he does not take firm grip of their attention in the first few minutes, how can he hope to hold it to the end?

It will be well if we settle our minds now about the question: Should one always take a text?

Not always! — but nearly always. The definition of preaching which we found nearest to the ideal (though, even then, not entirely comprehensive) laid down that it was "a manifestation of the Incarnate Word, *from the written Word.*" There will be times when a man must preach upon a theme without being able to give a textual indication of where he is working. He will be at all the greater pains on those rare occasions to make sure that he is in harmony with the whole tenor of the written Word, but he cannot pin his purpose down to a text. Let him announce his subject at those particular times with no opening reference to the Bible at all, but let his whole treatment of the theme leave his hearers in no doubt of his utter loyalty to the authority which all evangelical preachers accept.

We mentioned earlier that there are four common ways in which texts are treated in preaching. They can be:

1. The whole area of the sermon.
2. A genuine starting point for a subject it raises.
3. A "motto" — with a discernible relation to what is said.
4. A point of complete departure and used only of convention.

Let us look at this fourfold use of texts in greater detail.

The first use is pure exposition of the text. It is the high and sometimes hard task of making meaning clear. It specializes in the flavor of words and phrases. It deals with the nuance and with the overtone and undertone. It is the particular sphere of the linguistic scholar, though by no means his exclusive preserve. It aims to scoop the sense from the chosen phrase. Full success is achieved when the people depart after worship knowing clearly the purport of that fragment of Scripture and how it relates to their own daily lives.

The second use is not purely expository, though it is closely akin to it. The preacher takes a text and converts it into one pregnant phrase which expresses the subject of his sermon. The text and the phrase are closely related, though the phrase does not claim to be a whole exposition of everything in the text. It is an important subject suggested by the text, and the subject is the theme of all the preacher has to say; e.g.:

Text: "Behold, the handmaid of the Lord; be it unto me according to thy word." Luke 1:38.
Theme: Self-abandonment to the divine will.

Text: "Speak no more unto me of this matter." Deut. 3:26.

Theme: When God says, " No."

Text: "We are witnesses of these things; and so is the Holy Spirit, whom God hath given to them that obey him." Acts 5:32.

Theme: Obedience is the way to receive the Holy Spirit.

The legitimacy of the third use of a text I have distinguished is still warmly debated by the masters of our craft. There are those who hold (as I do myself) that the use of a text here is legitimate. There are others who argue that it comes to " twisting the Scriptures " and ought to be let alone.

It is not exposition. It cannot even be said that the chosen theme is *in* the text employed. There is a certain congruity between the phrase out of its context and the theme of the sermon, and those preachers who like a link at all times with the Holy Book make the connection and go ahead. I cannot condemn the practice just so long as the man knows what he is doing and lets his hearers know what he is doing too. John Wesley's sermon on " The Catholic Spirit " is a case in point. It is one of the noblest sermons he ever preached. It breathes a catholicity beyond the dreams of some who make more frequent use of the word; but it is no exposition of the text, and catholicity, in John Wesley's sense, is not even implied in it. He takes a text concerning Jehu: " And when he was departed thence, he lighted on Jehonadab the son of Rechab coming to meet him; and he saluted him, and said to him, Is thy heart right, as my heart is with thy heart? And Jehonadab answered, It is. If it be, give me thy hand." II Kings 10:15.

Wesley was honest with his hearers. He makes it quite

clear (par. 12) that he is not expounding the words as Jehu used them. He is well aware that Jehu is soaked in blood and possibly on his way to another massacre. Falling in with that fierce fanatic Jehonadab, Jehu sees the chance of making a useful ally, and the conversation has more to do with a cunning politician "using" a religious zealot than it has to do with catholicity.

Wesley was well aware of that, but he openly tossed that fact aside. Quoting the words, " Is thy heart right, as my heart is with thy heart? " he inquires, " What should a follower *of Christ* understand thereby, when he proposes it to any of his brethren? . . ." and all the sermon nobly answers that.

I say again that I do not think this practice illegitimate so long as everyone understands what is happening, but it should never be a common habit with a preacher. Regularly to treat Bible texts as pegs on which to hang our own ideas would be a sad misuse of the written Word.

The fourth use of a text is blatant mishandling of Scripture in a way no honest craftsman could condone. It does deliberate despite to the Word of God. It rips a phrase from its context and from the whole tenor of the Scriptures, and often uses it as a pretext for saying things that were not worth saying in the pulpit at any time. One wonders why men embarking on such a shabby enterprise take a text at all. Is it just convention? Do they hope to clothe their shallow thoughts in the majesty of Scripture? Are the devout to be deceived by such a soiled artifice?

One example of such unworthy work will be enough. I recall the instance of a German preacher, in the arid early years of the nineteenth century when the gospel had almost been lost in the land of Luther, announcing as his text one Easter morning: " Now on the first day of the week cometh Mary Magdalene early, while it was yet dark, unto the tomb," John 20:1. His theme was "The Benefits of Early Rising." He had nothing to say about the resurrection. He talked entirely to the tune, "It is nice to get up in the morning"!

Let us add as preachers another phrase to the liturgy: "From all mishandling of thy Holy Word, good Lord, deliver us."

We have admitted that there are rare occasions when a man is constrained to speak on a theme for which he cannot, however intimate his knowledge of Scripture, find an exact text or even a natural starting point. He might want to discuss the proper attitude of one denomination to another — but the New Testament has nothing directly to say upon that, if only because the Church, in settled divisions, was not so much as dreamed of in New Testament times. Or the preacher might want to raise the question with his people, "Is it our duty as Christians to support the United Nations?" and, again, no natural text might leap to his mind.

Let him go ahead without one. So long as the teaching of the Bible overarches all he says, and the clear orientation of his sermon is always to God and God's will, it is enough. God will honor his faithfulness and the Word will not return void.

The announcement of a text, however, does not settle the question of how the sermon actually begins. It is true that a preacher has nothing better to give to his congregation than his text, but, having given it, that vital matter of the start still confronts him. How shall he begin? By what means can he make sure that the mild, or more than mild, interest of the people shall not be thrown away but held, deepened, excited, inflamed even?

The beginning of the sermon has already been determined in part by the structural type. The kind of porch, if any, that the house will have is normally fixed by the architectural style you adopt. Not all houses have, or need, a lodge gate and a long drive up to the door. Not all have a porch or a " hall." Into many cottage homes you can step in a stride from the street to the fireside — and useful dwellings many of them are.

The idea of some preachers that all sermons must have an " introduction " is nonsense. If the subject demands it, it must have it, but be glad when it is quite unnecessary and you can step swiftly in. Years ago I used to pass on my way to my church a wee house with an enormous porch. I see it in my mind's eye as I write. Great Corinthian pillars complete with acanthus leaves supported a baroque portico which would have given shelter from the rain for half a platoon of soldiers. On the other side of this enormous porch was something like the cheapest kind of council house. I always smiled as I went by. It reminded me of two things: the man who began to build and had not wherewith to finish, and, also, certain sermons I have heard. All introduction! Ornate splendor round the door . . . and next to nothing on the other side! The little house by itself could be warm and welcoming and snug. But after that ridiculous porch!

It is a parable. There are small sermons. Minor duties must receive pulpit emphasis at times. But they do not remain small when they are related to God. Sweeping a room for him and his laws, George Herbert tells us, " makes . . . the action fine." But those sermons do not call for elaborate porches. Just get in!

The way in which structural type and psychological method determine the start is clear on a moment's reflection. If the sermon argues a case and is persuasive in method, the thesis must be quickly announced and some

indication given of the road that is to be traveled. One
need not give a detailed map of the whole route at the
beginning; some surprises can be left to the journey itself.
But the main route must be plain: "We are going *there!*
I want you all to come with me."

If, on the other hand, one is raising some question
of Christian philosophy and employing the co-operative
method, one cannot announce where one is going. The
method forbids. We — preacher and people — are looking
for the answer together. Something of perplexity must
mark the clear setting-out of the problem, though something of hope as we all begin the search.

Both methods of beginning, of course, have their dangers. It is fine, in a way, to know from the start what the
preacher is after and the route he means to take, yet it
can be very boring to look down a straight road for three
miles and find nothing inviting in view. Some element of
surprise must be kept in reserve when the route is known,
but, more than this, the theme itself must not be obvious.
If a man chooses to argue a thesis that nobody contests, he
is almost certainly doomed to dullness from the start. The
argumentative structure and persuasive method is normally called for by some message not easy to receive, or a
truth that even a Christian congregation may be inclined
at times to doubt. If, therefore, a man announces that he
will grapple with a certain problem that obviously strains
faith, the people need to know what he is seeking to do
and are glad of an early indication of the route. They are
ready to set out with him because the wonder is in their
mind: "Can he prove it? Is it in the Scriptures? Is it confirmed in experience?" But marshaling arguments to prove
what is either obvious or does not matter anyhow is foolish
in essence and begins in the same boredom with which it
will surely end.

On the other hand, the danger a man is in who pro-
pounds a really perplexing problem but employs the co-
operative method is not less real, and it meets him as
surely at the beginning as it meets the man who works the
other way. Unless he takes swift and firm grip, and can
get the people aware of the problem to be solved, and
aware also of its importance to them, they will be wondering all the time what he is after. Unless he has pace right
from the beginning, and makes fairly swift transitions to
quite real " discoveries " of the way out, the clouds will
thicken about that bewildered congregation and, not
knowing where they are really starting, they will know
neither the route nor the end.

If we keep both these dangers in mind, the sailing chan-
nel between them will be plain. Like the modest pilot to
whom the gushing passenger remarked, " You must know
every rock and sandbank in this estuary," we can quietly
answer: " I don't. I know only where the deep water is."

But having made it plain that the beginning of the
sermon is really determined for us already by the structural type and psychological method we choose to employ, let us look at what are, in point of fact, common and
legitimate ways to begin.

Some reference to the setting of the text is often called
for. It is especially called for in exposition. Ripping a text
from a sentence or paragraph is a dangerous occupation
at any time. It is dubious if any other book than the Bible
would be treated in that way. Moreover, while the versi-
fication of the Bible, as most students will agree, was a
necessary piece of mechanism for its close study and wide
reference, yet it shared little of the inspiration that attended the writing of the book itself. Verse endings and
chapter endings come, at times, in most grotesque posi-

tions, and it was no small service on the part of the re-
visers to put the Bible back into the paragraphings of its
own sense.

Even so, the expositor, in taking his verse or phrase, is
usually compelled to relate it to what went before. Honest
dealing with the Word and with the people requires it.
But let it be done swiftly. The tedious repetition in one's
own words of the whole passage (which the people probably heard ten minutes before as one of the lessons) is a
waste of time and a waste of their precious interest. One
cannot grip that way — and these are the moments to grip.

His context made clear, the expositor can move swiftly
to the actual elucidation of the phrase he has chosen to
expound.

Now let us assume that it is not an expository sermon,
but one in which the text is employed to suggest a theme.
The announcement of the theme must come as quickly as
possible. Indeed, some able preachers make a practice of
announcing their text and saying at once, " My subject
is . . ." They give the theme in their first phrase. No small
part of their toilsome preparation has been the making of
that one fecund phrase. They announce it, therefore, right
away and the sermon has begun. No winding drive to the
front door. No porch. They step in.

The difference between the man who starts with his
context and the man who starts with his subject is often
related to a deeper difference than has appeared as yet.
It may indicate the way they want to work. If it is possible
to begin in Ur of the Chaldees and end in London, it is
just as legitimate to begin in Birmingham and end in
Jerusalem. One can work from the normal facts of our
day-to-day life, but arrive at the green hill " without a
city wall." Or one can begin at the place of the skull and
end with Tom Smith flying the Atlantic in a plane.

Let us suppose that a man is preaching on faith. He can begin by asserting that "all life is by faith." He can point out the absurdity of supposing that faith belongs only to religion. Faith belongs to getting on a bus — faith that the driver is really capable. Faith belongs to going into a restaurant — faith that the food is wholesome and all it pretends to be. Faith belongs to sending the children to school — faith that the teacher will not hang evil pictures on the walls of their minds or curse them with some terrible inferiority. Faith belongs to getting married — faith in the one you choose to be the lifelong mate of all your joys and sorrows. Faith culminates in religion.

Up and up the preacher goes! From earth to heaven. From a bus ride to the beatific vision. It is a legitimate path to take; it has the great merit of starting where the people are. Do they not all use buses? But it gets, at the last, to an empty tomb and an ascended Christ.

Yet the preacher could have worked precisely the other way. He could have begun, not on a bus in London, but in a caravan at Ur of the Chaldees. He could begin with the text, "Abraham . . . went out, not knowing whither he went," Heb. 11:8, and he could sketch with clean, deft strokes the great renunciation all those centuries ago of a man truly sensitive to the touch of the living God. Much is known of Ur now. All the material is there. "See him going! Where? He doesn't know! Why? God has called him. He goes in *faith*."

Beginning at Ur of the Chaldees, the preacher can end in Manchester, Leeds, or Birmingham, with some young man or woman giving his or her heart to God and starting on the pilgrim way.

And again the method is permissible. One way has the advantage of beginning where the people are. The other has the advantage of ending where the people are. The second method, with such a theme as faith, intrigues the most hesitant preacher of evangelism to say, "Come." Both ways have their merits and wise men employ them both.

We promised, however, to discuss in more fullness at this stage what is called "life-situation preaching." We took the view that this is not a new kind of preaching either in subject matter or in structural type, nor in psychological method. In subject matter it is normally ethical; in structural type it is usually argumentative; in psychological method it is almost always co-operative.

Nonetheless, it is a combination among our classifications that is full of interest and practical worth. It is treated here because it is essentially a starting point, and a gripping one at that.

The exponents of life-situation preaching are often critical of pure exposition. They are *too* critical. In pressing their own approach they have rendered a real service. In supposing that their approach is the only one they go grievously wrong.

They criticize a man who begins with the setting of his text on the ground that the congregation has not the slightest interest in Abraham, Isaac, Jacob, or any other Old Testament character. "While you are dawdling in the past, and getting excited in your professional way over scraps of Hebrew history, the attention of your people is already slipping. Those men and women in front of you are nearly all facing problems. One woman has begun a dangerous liaison with a married man. That widow is seething with resentment because her only son wants to get married. That man works for an irate boss who expects him to lie for him on occasion. That girl is smoldering with sex and has begun to think that her past firmness in moral conviction is only prudery and that she will miss her

chance of being wed unless she is more free with the boys.
. . . A problem in nearly every pew. Face them! Face
them one by one! Start your sermon by sketching the problem. It is not a theoretical problem. It is practical, living,
urgent. That is where people want your help. Even when
you are dealing with a problem that is not his own, every
man will feel the thrust of your words upon someone else,
and will long for the answer. Bring preaching close to life.
That is the urgent need today. Nothing so much as this
would make the pulpit powerful once more. . . ."

We need not agree with everything that is said here to
concede that a case has been made out. The preaching
that never deals with " life situations " is sadly remote
from life, and every man facing the same congregation
regularly should remember this way of approach. The
sermon begins with the problem in a picture: " I read in
the newspaper last week . . ." " A man said to me the
other day . . ." " Before I entered the ministry, and when
I was in business life, I was once faced with this situation . . ." There it is! It must not be so plain, of course,
that other people in the congregation could at once iden-
tify the pew in which the living problem sat, but vital
and common enough to be of interest to all, and not easy
of solution. Grapple with that! The people will sit up as
you set it out, and hang with eagerness on the words of
any man who has a satisfying answer. It does not begin
with the Bible, even though a text may have been announced, but, if it is well done, the tie-up with the Bible
is plain before the sermon comes to its close. If the answer is given clearly, fearlessly, and yet tenderly, all are
grateful. The person whose actual problem it is will remember that sermon until the day of his death.

The gains of this way of beginning can easily be set out.
One does not need to *get* the people's attention: one is so

close to life that one has it already. Moreover, the needs
of people cry aloud for this kind of specific help. Many
magazines and periodicals employ a personal adviser, who
invites the readers to write and pose their particular problems. The replies are often published, and while they
are kind and well-meaning, they are seldom radical or
adequate, and there is hardly any mention of God. Yet
almost all real problems are problems of religion in the
end. If the needs of people were being met in an adequate
way in the pulpits, these anxious people would receive
much more effective help. Nor do the gains end here. The
bias of some men in preaching is always to deal with vast
questions. Unaware of it probably themselves, they paint
always on an immense canvas, and world affairs occupy
their whole thought. Dealing in the pulpit with personal
problems would keep these preachers nearer to the people, and nearer to individual need. A devout American
told me once that through a period of grave anxiety in his
life he went to church Sunday after Sunday and heard
every single morning some aspect of Britain's mishandling
of India discussed in the pulpit: Mr. Gandhi, the poor
Moslems, the outcastes, infant mortality, the wages of tea
pickers — never a word matched to his personal need.
There are preachers like that in England too, and the cure
for them in both continents is a more frequent use of that
method of preaching which grapples with personal problems and keeps a man's feet on the earth. If, in the solution of the problems, a man has knowledge and skill
enough to employ the insights and techniques that Christian psychology has placed at his hand, his usefulness under God can hardly be measured. He will avoid, of course,
the jargon of psychology, and avoid also the impression
of merely " using " religion to attain certain states of mental well-being, but, in its subordinate place, psychology

will serve his ends. Especially in those sermons that we classified as "How to" sermons will he find it of constant use. The precise explanation of the way to achievement utilizes all our knowledge of the workings of the human mind.

The dangers of "life-situation preaching" must be watched as well. It can easily become too humanistic — savoring more of psychology than of religion, and more of Samuel Smiles's *Self-help* than of the Bible. Preaching is never Christian preaching if it does not center in God and in his disclosure of himself in Jesus. Moreover, men can become so fascinated with this one method that they can ride it to death, never lifting the eyes of their people to wider horizons, nor forcing them to face large social problems or deep doctrinal truths. Men have even slipped into the foolish error of starting a sermon with a problem they could not solve themselves, and putting problems into people's minds that were never there until they thrust them in. Personal problems can never be the whole of a congregation's diet. There are not enough of them (thank God!) for fifty-two Sundays year after year — and if there were, they would leave people terribly preoccupied with themselves. Imagine it! No exposition of the word; no high doctrine; none of the deeper philosophic problems; no evangelism! "Life-situation preaching" is a way of beginning practical ethical sermons, and a good way. It has its unmistakable place in our study, but it must be resolutely kept in its place.

Is it possible for us now to affirm anything about the beginning of all sermons? Howsoever we start, are there particular canons concerning the opening that should ever be borne in mind?

There are three, and they are quite general. They have

been latent in much that we have already said, but they can be pulled into sharper focus now. The beginning of the sermon (the "introduction" as the more formal preachers called it) should be:

1. *Brief*

We have admitted that some sermons require an introduction. It is just not possible to step into every subject in a phrase, but the introduction must be as short as it possibly can. One must labor, if necessary, to have it so. Cut into the subject with sharp, terse phrases. Resist, as you would resist the devil, that awful tendency to drag. Let the people feel in your whole manner that you have something most important to say and you simply cannot waste words: " Here is a man covetous of every moment he has." That spirit does not militate against a decent reverence and cannot be confused with rush and breathlessness at " the throne of the Word of God."

2. *Interesting*

There are still people about who suppose that the duller the sermon the holier it is. Not many of them are in the pews. Whatever some preachers think, the people are right who cling pathetically to the conviction that preaching ought to be interesting. Parts of it will be hard, no doubt. To justify the ways of God to men cannot, in the nature of things, be easy, nor easily understood, but that is the preacher's job. Can the truth impress the mind and affect the life unless it is understood and received? Can it be understood and received if it is not made interesting?

It must be made interesting — and nowhere more interesting than when it begins. Howsoever a man may start, let him make sure that his opening sentences have grappling irons: something cast out and taking firm hold of the minds of his hearers: something which will make them say to him in their hearts when he pauses: " Go on! Go on! "

3. *Arresting*

It will not always be possible to achieve this, and one ought not constantly to try to achieve it in the same way. One must have variety here as elsewhere in preaching, and " shock " tactics can be overdone.

Yet people can be arrested sharply by other than " shock " tactics. There is the piquant opening. A sharp paradox can arrest. An incisive question thrust at the heart of the text the moment it is uttered can do it. It can be done by contradicting the text immediately, from the superficial standpoint of worldly wisdom, and then fighting back to the Bible truth again. Or, if one does not contradict it, one can cast doubt upon it in an opening phrase. None of these are oratorical " tricks." They have been called that by the lazy and incapable, but *their* praise is criticism and their criticism praise. The serious craftsman can afford to ignore such comments. He has the awful task of making the Word of God live to men and women who have been busy all the week seeking the bread of this life and who, even in the sanctuary, find it hard to keep their minds on God and holy things. He must help them in every wholesome way he can. If he can get an arresting beginning, he may have their awed attention the whole time and be able securely to hide the truth of God deep in their hearts.

Few who heard J. N. Figgis preach his last sermon before the University of Cambridge ever forgot the way he began. It was June 2, 1918. After nearly four years of grueling war, the Allies were being driven back again. Miles that had taken months to win were lost in hours. In that tense atmosphere of national fear he started with the text: "The Lord sitteth upon the flood; yea, the Lord sitteth King for ever" (Ps. 29:10, K.J.V.), and he began at once with one tense question: "*Does he? Does he?*" That was enough. He was in.

They still tell at Princeton University of the visit of Sparhawk Jones to their chapel and his announcement of the text: "Is thy servant a dog, that he should do this thing?" (II Kings 8:13, K.J.V.). After a moment's pause, he began crisply: "Dog or no dog, he did it!"

Those are two excellent examples of a good beginning. Perhaps it would not be altogether inappropriate to sharpen the point by two examples of how *not* to begin. It was an expositional sermon of the Twenty-third Psalm. The preacher began: "This psalm is written from the viewpoint of a sheep!" Quite true — but utterly banal! I cannot even recall the text of the other sermon whose beginning I have in mind, but it does not matter. It was probably the worst opening of a sermon in all history: "I feel I have a feeling which I feel you feel as well!"

VI

The Conclusion of the Sermon

IT IS an idle question whether the beginning or the end of a sermon is more important. If you do not get the people's attention, nothing you say will make any difference. If you get their attention and do not put it to the highest use, you will have failed to make the occasion "a maximum for God."

So impressed are some teachers of homiletics with the importance of the beginning and end of the sermon that, though they wisely advise against *memoriter* preaching, they counsel unpracticed beginners to memorize both the opening and the closing sentences of all they plan to say.

The importance of the conclusion can best be seen in this way. Every sermon should have not only a subject but an *object*. It must aim to do something, something quite precise, something that can be written out in a few plain words before the immediate preparation of the sermon begins. In expository preaching, the aim is to make clear the meaning of a text or a passage. In ethical preaching, it is to make the people thrill over a particular virtue or grace, and not merely to thrill about it, but to long for it and study to secure it in their own hearts; or, conversely, to make them loathe a particular vice, turn from it, and scheme to become its master. In devotional, philosophic, social, or evangelistic preaching, the aim is no less clear. Stop any able preacher on his way to his pulpit and ask him what he plans to do that morning and you will have a crisp reply; ask his people when they are dispersing after worship and they will tell you no less plainly that he has done it.

Consequently, there can never be any uncertainty in able preaching where the sermon will " come out." There is nothing haphazard about it. Free as the man is to receive the help of the Holy Spirit in the act of preaching, it is normally a help to do what the Holy Spirit has already inspired him to do in the quiet of his own preparation. God is not a God of vagaries. To suggest, as some men do, that it limits the Holy Spirit if we know the precise purpose of a sermon before we begin to preach is surely nonsense. The inspiration of the Holy Spirit does not belong only to the hour of the sermon's utterance. He it is who inspires the original purpose in the heart of a man who has sought guidance before he begins. The immediate help the preacher receives in the hour of preaching is that he may better do what God has already made plain that he should do. That dreadful vagueness which hangs over so much preaching derives in the main from the fact that it is not clearly aiming to *do* something. The preacher himself has no clear object in view. It is not a matter for wonder, therefore, that the people also find it painfully vague.

A few years ago, Representative Woodrum in the Congress of the United States was discussing an economy measure, and he argued that, while everybody wanted economy, nobody seemed able to say precisely where. He illustrated his point with a story of a Negro preacher. For years the good man had been trying to point the way to a better life, but his congregation remained unappreciative and unimpressed. Finally, the governing body of the church decided that they had better find a new preacher. The Negro pastor, when he learned the decision, protested vigorously.

" Ain't I challenged the devil? " he asked the chairman of the committee.

" You shore has challenged the devil," agreed the chairman.

" Don't I argufy the Scriptures? "

" You shore does argufy the Scriptures."

" And don't I disputify the Scriptures? Tell me, brother, what am de trouble? "

The chairman scratched his head and explained: " Well, parson, it's this way. You challenges the devil all right; you argufies the Scriptures fine; and you shore disputifies the Scriptures. But the trouble with you is, you don't *specify wherein.*"

Many, many preachers fail to " specify wherein." It is impossible to " specify wherein " unless one has a clear object in view. How can one be definite if one does not know what one is going to be definite about?

When the object is clear from the beginning, one knows what the conclusion must be. The sermon is as direct a path as possible to that conclusion. Clearly, therefore, the conclusion will never be " stuck on." It is an integral part of the whole. It is jointed. All else has led up to it. As soon trace a lighting circuit through a dark room and find no bulb at the end as preach a sermon with no natural and fitting conclusion. What is the purpose of it, if not that? Is it not to give light at the last, an adequate light? — not a great cable concluding with a fifteen-watt lamp, but a bulb matched to the supply and matched to the chamber it must flood with light.

Some preachers have " detachable " conclusions which are added (it would almost seem by chance) to anything they have been saying. One of these is often a general exhortation for " the Spirit of Christ " (which normally means next to nothing when it can be tacked on to anything) and could have appeared as naturally or unnaturally, and certainly as uselessly, at the end of half the sermons they ever preach. Or else they urge their congregations to " go on; right on! ", though they have given no indication where, nor why, nor how. They have no real end in view. It flatters them to say that they have " shot an arrow into the air." It was certainly " into the air," but it had none of the point or speed of the arrow. It is highly dubious if, years after, there will be any happy sequel such as attended the man who cast his song into the air. It is more than doubtful if any part of that sermon will ever be found in the hearts of those who heard it.

So important is the conclusion of the sermon that some keen craftsmen prepare it first. They know the danger of putting a disproportionate amount of time into the beginning and scamping the conclusion, so they work first on what the folk will hear last. I share their sense of the conclusion's importance without approving their order of preparation. It is better, when the hours of immediate preparation come, to work from beginning to end. Although one knows what one is aiming to do, one cannot know until the actual preparation *just* where the " joint " for the conclusion will come. Transitions from one part of a sermon to another have to be handled with skill, and no little art is called for in securing an easy " runover." It will be simpler to find if one's preparation follows the logical sequence of thought.

But, if one does not take the heroic course of preparing the conclusion first, one must make utterly sure that it has adequate part of the preparation. After all, the whole sermon was leading up to this. If this is not done well, to what purpose all the previous labor? Few things are more annoying in a sermon than to hear a man say, when he is coming to the hard or important part, " Time fails me," and then simply blunt the thing off. Quite often, it is not even honest. One has heard men say it in broadcast addresses. They have known precisely how long they were expected to speak. They have a typescript before them. They have "timed" their effusions more than once and to the half minute — but here they are, when the people are most expectant, pleading that the absence of time prevents them passing on the golden thoughts that would have made all the difference. The sad truth is that the matter had not been wrought out in their own minds. They had less than little to drive home. Everything has led up to nothing. They have only advertised the unfinished character of their thought.

It reminds one of the unhandy man in the home who decides to hang a picture. All the family must help. One brings the ladder, another the hammer, while a third must step back to agree upon the right place on the wall. The great moment has come. With two of the household supporting the ladder, he mounts the steps complete with hammer, puts his finger on the precise and agreed spot — and then discovers that he has no nail!

Even when a man is quite honest in pleading that he has been beaten by the clock, it is still poor workmanship. He should have arranged his matter better. If he had jettisoned an illustration earlier, and avoided that tempting bypath, we should not now be in this state of disappointment. Nor do the early merits of the sermon redeem its truncated end. In a sense, they increase it. The better the beginning, the sharper the disappointment in its abrupt termination. It would not matter so much if it were a picture sermon or an analogy. But to raise a hard problem and neither solve it nor show the way to its solving is quite shocking in a preacher. Of that sermon it could truly be said, "It were better if it had never been born."

Let every preacher, therefore, lay this canon to heart: The conclusion must not be scamped. It must not be scamped in preparation; it must not be scamped in delivery. It need not be said, of course, that it should not be padded. Nothing in a sermon can be padded.

But conclusions (unlike beginnings) are often *too* short. Twenty-five minutes of argument and a phrase or two for conclusion is disproportionate. Without wasting words, the sermon must receive a masterly finish, and fall with satisfying completeness on the ear and mind of all who have intelligently followed it.

It is possible for us now to discuss the various kinds of conclusion which we may give to a sermon. Not all conclusions need be the same. The wholesome freshness we have sought in all aspects of our study must be our aim here also. The subject matter of the sermon and the architectural type employed will inevitably affect the end. An ethical sermon will normally conclude differently from a sermon in apologetics. A sermon that has argued will not finish in the same way as one that has put the truth in pictures. No hard exclusiveness will control all this. As we have seen before, it adds to the infinite variety of preaching to combine subject matter, and architectural types, and psychological methods, in novel ways. So long as the conclusion is the fitting one, and firmly jointed to the main structure, we may expect that some skill in adaptability will give us variety here also.

But let us look at some of the commonest ways of bringing the sermon to an end.

1. *Recapitulation*

This is normally called for in sermons that have argued. The argument may have been difficult in parts. A line of reasoning, which has become familiar to the preacher by long preparatory brooding, is falling with freshness on the ear of the people. They are tracing the path as the preacher picks it out, but it is a step at a time. If the route was especially complex, the wise preacher glanced back more than once on the way, making it clear to the people how far we had reached "up to *this* point." But now he has come to the end. The backward glance must extend to the whole road. A map without detail must be held up before them. We have journeyed from A to F — and with swift, terse phrases he recapitulates the route again. He uses not one redundant word. The journey is plain before them and the inevitability of the conclusion is plain also. The logic is so constraining that the keenest intelligence cannot resist it. The case is complete, and completely satisfying. The recapitulation ends with the truth snug in the minds of the people, and the sermon stops at once.

2. *Application*

Some preachers suppose that all sermons must have an application, but, if the word is given any sharpness of meaning, that is quite mistaken. Application in homiletics means the pointed relation of the truth newly expressed to the lives of the people immediately in front of the preacher.

Not all sermons are capable of that pointed and personal application. The aim of some preaching is to cast light on large problems. The sermon achieves its end when people better understand the problem, but it may leave them with no immediate duty that they must arise and do. A sermon on the philosophical approach to religion may gloriously nourish faith in hard-pressed people, but, again, it leaves no immediate duty to be done and calls for no "application" in the proper sense of the word. Even an evangelical sermon does not demand an application unless one so describes its culminating appeal, "Come!"

Applications belong rather to ethical and devotional sermons, and to such expository and doctrinal preaching as leads a man to say to his congregation: "If this be true, what does it mean for you and me? It means . . ." The application follows at once. Its omission then would be fatal to that kind of preaching. The line of thought demands it. It must be as concrete, as direct, and as pointed as possible.

All preaching gains when it has a concrete duty with which to conclude. As we have already seen, it is not always possible or necessary to conclude with clear duties, but no practiced preacher will deny that he comes nearest to the people in conclusions that require a personal application. He says, "You . . ." He looks the people in the face and presses the point into their hearts and minds. In these last moments of his sermon, every phrase is a stroke hammering the truth home. Nothing is clearer to the people than the things they have now to do themselves. Indeed, as the service reaches its awesome end, there is an impatience in them to get away and translate the truth into life. The deep impression demands a full expression. The application has done its work.

3. *Demonstration*

There are some sermons that we have classified as "How to" sermons. Their *whole* matter is "How to." A desirable end is announced in the first few moments and the complete message is given to showing how that end may be achieved. But many sermons that are not wholly "How to" require a "How to" termination. To hold up to admiration some lovely and winsome grace and end without indicating how it may be achieved is disappointing to the people. It is not much more helpful if the conclusion is abbreviated into a phrase or two exhorting them to pray for the coveted thing. The preacher is not specific enough. Has he not learned from life or the saints some simple technique of achievement? Can he not be concrete and detailed and say, "Do this; do that"? If, at the end of his efforts to explain, he has clearly not explained it all, well, we can leave something to the grace of God but, at least, we know where to begin.

Few terminations are more practically helpful than these. No preacher need feel unduly depressed if his efforts to be specific here often leave him aware that the half has not been told. He will strive, of course, to get as near to completeness as possible, but his real difficulty lies in the very nature of the soul's commerce with God. It is impossible fully to put in a set of rules the mystic ways in which God conveys grace to the soul. We may be glad that it is so. God aids us in ways we *cannot* explain. The best we can do is to help people get into paths where aid is most likely to come. Just how it comes, we do not fully know. Still less can we tell others. We employ " the language of solids," and " the language of solids " is too heavy for this delicate elucidation.

But the effort and a partial success here mean so much. It is one of the rare cases where sixty per cent of achievement may be taken as a maximum.

4. *Illustration*

A sermon is sometimes effectively concluded with an illustration. Such an end can serve any type of construction, though it would be least effective or needed in biographical preaching (where the events of the life itself are a source of constant illustration), or in picture preaching (which is a catena of illustration), or in analogy (which is a complete illustration from beginning to end). But an expositional sermon, or an argument, can reach a fine conclusion this way. The meaning has been quarried from the text, or the flinty piece of reasoning has been worked to its fitting end, and the time has come to close. The people are a little tired, maybe, from thirty minutes of serious thinking, and yet one cannot part from them without gathering it all up for its final reception into their believing hearts.

Put it in an illustration. Hold up a picture that will both recapitulate and apply all that is in your mind. Having given the illustration, end! Make the illustration so good that it is utterly unnecessary to add more than a concluding sentence or two afterward — and be glad when it does not even require that.

A sermon had been exposing the evil done by false spiritual guides and the stress had fallen on the uniqueness of Jesus as Saviour. The new moralists, together with the psychologists and scientists who belong to the antireligious schools, had all received attention, but the fact had to be faced that many false guides are sincere guides. They cannot do what they claim to do, but they really think they can. Therein lies the tragedy of it. Although they honestly believe they can save, you will follow them nonetheless at your peril.

The sermon had a terse illustrative end:

"A few years ago, during 'Navy Week' at Plymouth, the festivities were spoiled by a distressing accident. A young sailor was put up to demonstrate a new and wonderful lifesaving apparatus and, in the midst of the demonstration, something went wrong and he lost his life.

"The irony of it! He was demonstrating a lifesaving apparatus and he *lost* his life.

"Spiritual quacks are like that. They claim to have a soul-saving method, but you will follow it at your peril. 'None but Jesus can do helpless sinners good.'"

On another occasion a sermon had dealt with the recollection of divine sonship in the soul of all men. The argument had been sustained and illustrated, but it required a final, vivid picture before the close. It was essential for the people to see that no man is utterly lost who knows where he really belongs. The conclusion was found in this personal experience of the preacher.

"Some time ago a poor drunkard committed his life to Christ in this church. Twenty years before he had been a church official in the Midlands, but he came to London, took to drink, and drifted to the gutter. When he capitulated to Christ, he had a pathetic hope that his thirst might be quenched by some stroke of omnipotence.

"It wasn't!

"There began that day a long guerrilla warfare in his soul between the deadly craving and the keeping power of Christ.

"As his new friend, I suggested that, on any day in which he found the fight especially hard, he might drop in and we could have prayer together. He dropped in often. His drawn face told its own story. We would go into the chapel and pray.

"One day, as I was praying with him, he broke down completely. The contrast between his earlier life of holy service and the revolting bestiality to which drunkenness had brought him was too much. He sobbed like a child and said: 'I know I'm in the gutter. I *know* it. But, oh, I don't belong there, do I? Tell me, I don't belong there!'

"I put my arm around him. I felt a great elation even in the pain and embarrassment of his tears. He had lost his way, but not his address.

"'No,' I said quite positively, 'you don't belong there. You belong to God.'"

5. Peroration

Originally, the word "peroration" simply meant "speaking from beginning to end," but it came to be used especially for the concluding part of a speech or sermon, and more recently it has acquired an unpleasant flavor.

It now describes a conclusion of a certain kind, and hence invites our separate notice here.

To perorate today means to conclude with a rhetorical flourish. The speaker or preacher "works himself up." He is on the last lap and the tape is coming into view. Quite often he shouts. His gestures increase in number and vehemence. The congregation become gratefully aware that he will not last much longer and mentally prepare to go. Down the last stretch of the track he thunders. He usually passes the finishing post with a bit of memorized poetry, and when he ends there is a great calm.

Do not perorate. The custom must be dropped, not mainly because it is old-fashioned, but because the emotion is faked. It is not suggested for a moment that men who perorate are insincere. The number of really insincere men in the pulpit must be negligible. It is the emotion that is insincere. The man *believes* what he says. No doubt he would die for his beliefs, but, quite frankly, he is not feeling any tidal wave of emotion at that moment, though he feels that he ought to. Hence the "working up." One can almost hear the cranking at times, and it may start so suddenly as to give the impression that the speaker has a mark on his notes of the point where the steam pressure should be turned on. Public opinion, both in churches and outside them, has rightly turned against the peroration, and, whenever it represents counterfeited feeling, one hopes that it will never come back.

Particularly is this true of the pulpit. Nothing that savors of the unreal can be permitted here. When a man is full of feeling on a point that he is making, let him speak out and spare not; if gesticulation is a natural expression of his personality, let him move hand and arm as he will to emphasize and illustrate his meaning; but to *pretend* to emotion is bad in a preacher and sickening to people. It makes an actor of the man of God — and the words " ac-

tor " and " hypocrite " are etymologically too near together
to leave the conscience comfortable. Emotion can be felt
and expressed without perorating. Some of the most intense moments at the end of a sermon are quiet moments
— and all the more moving because they are so quiet. One
expects to be at a high moment when one comes to the
end of the sermon, but never let the expression of feeling
outrun the honest awareness of it. Rising declamation has
its honorable time in preaching, when the tide of feeling in
a preacher's heart demands a vent that way. Emotion
in preaching is really aroused and unconsciously " stored "
in the preparation to preach. It comes as one broods on the
message in prayer and becomes thrillingly aware that this
is a message from God. One may go to the pulpit completely calm, but, in the act of preaching, that thrilling
remembrance suddenly flares up again. Then it is genuine
and noble feeling. Let it surge out as it will. Coming that
way, it will bring with it all the justification that it needs.

These, then, are the five ways in which sermons com-
monly end. They are not mutually exclusive. They can
combine in many ways. Recapitulation and application can
blend. Demonstration can be given by illustration. Respect for these classified ends must never militate against
clarity, concreteness, or force. The end should be a high
moment in the sermon — normally, the highest of all.
Powerfully achieve that, and no theorist in preaching will
take you to task.

But certain warnings should be uttered before we finish
our discussion of the conclusion of the sermon, and they
would be best uttered here.

Do not, in coming to the conclusion of the sermon, have
the air of the militant moralist who had told his improv-
ing tale and reached the stage, " Now the lesson of all

this . . ." How we hated that moment when we were children, and in the hands of an unskillful Sunday school teacher! Every story had that wretched addendum, and the warning phrase was the signal for general fidgeting. The deep way to avoid the trouble is to be sure that one has a "jointed" and integral conclusion. It is the "stuck on" variety of termination that is most exposed to this final inattention because the interest is not really running over and holding the people to the last word.

Do not make the conclusion of the sermon the conclusion only of the last point — except where the last point is itself climactic. It is true that in a sermon cut by faceting, and also in a sermon made orderly by categorizing, a partial summary and application are natural and necessary at the end of each section, but when the conclusion of the whole is reached, it should conclude *the whole*. The relations of the earlier points must be shortly and skillfully tied up with the last one. The people must see that it is a whole. The unity of the sermon must be clear in its final moments and a grand sense of completeness must lie in their minds.

Do not announce that you are concluding — or not often, and never twice in the same sermon. How wearisome it is to run with a flatulent preacher through the whole gamut of " Finally . . . ; Lastly . . . ; In conclusion . . . ," and still have another seven minutes to go! It is amazing how many synonyms can be found for "finally." It is best to avoid all these stimulations of hope (!) and run right on to that clear conclusion that has been in your eye from the moment you set out. Occasionally, when a man has strained his people's thinking with a hard piece of analysis, but wants a final effort from them before he concludes, he may be forgiven for saying, " A minute more," and, if they know he keeps his word when he asks for that minute, they will gladly give it to him. But keep to the minute! — and do not make a practice even of asking that.

Do not introduce new matter into a conclusion. It is too late! You need these precious final moments for recapitulation, or application, or demonstration, but not for starting their minds off on new tracks. It is positively harmful to introduce fresh lines of thought now. They will militate for attention against the positions already won. However good that point might have been had it come in earlier, throw it away now. It is the emphasis and establishment of everything already said that is your concern in these moments, and you must allow nothing to divert you from that single aim.

Having come to the end, stop. Do not cruise about looking for a spot to land, like some weary swimmer coming in from the sea and splashing about until he can find a shelving beach up which to walk. Come right in, and land at once. Finish what you have to say and end at the same time. If the last phrase can have some quality of crisp memorableness, all the better, but do not grope even for that. Let your sermon have the quality that Charles Wesley coveted for his whole life: let the work and the course end together.

Be vigilant to see that any final metaphor you use does not have an overtone of banality. A friend of mine heard a preacher at a watch-night service work out a not ineffective address on the thrill of turning over to a clean sheet. All through the sermon the clean-sheet metaphor echoed again and again. He perorated a little at the close and thundered to a conclusion with a dramatic gesture and this final exhortation, " Go home! — and begin the New Year with clean sheets! "

VII
Methods of Preparation

IT IS possible that a student has read this book so far with the growing wonder that the comparatively simple task of preaching a sermon should seem as complicated as it has sometimes appeared here. It is certain that many preachers, with years of experience, might grow impatient with my theorizing and declare that they have practiced the art with no small success and never considered structural types, psychological method, and much else that it has seemed important to me to discuss.

I am not without sympathy in their bewilderment. I did not study, first, the theory of preaching myself, and then begin its practice; but preached because I felt God had given me a message and I should know no peace until it was said. Indeed, the writing of this manual has not been the recollection of early lectures on homiletics, because my college course included none, but rather a questioning of my own mind to learn what principles had, in fact, governed my work for thirty years and the clear enunciation of which might save time for other men.

Consequently, I do not picture to myself a person approaching this holy vocation having vowed not to preach until he has mastered the theory, and then sitting down to the task of making his first sermon with his mind held by the difference between an Aristotelian and a Goclenian sorites, and oscillating over the authoritative or subversive psychological method — or anything else that was honestly important to note. Here, as elsewhere, *solvitur ambulando*. We learn by doing. Preaching teaches us how to preach. Unless I am vastly mistaken, the theory is immensely valuable, but its study must be accompanied by constant practice, and the one will aid and illustrate the other. Let the theory lie deep in the mind. Use it *after* preaching to analyze what you have said and how you have said it. These " post-mortems " on sermons will have their high and unconscious influence on all your subsequent efforts. But when you are actually preparing to preach, fix the mind, not on your theories, but on this practical task: " What must I say? How best can I say it? " Some recourse to theory, no doubt, you will make in your preparation — but only occasionally. The theory will help most in *subtle* ways. Focus the aim! " How can I do *that?* " Bend all your efforts to the immediate and practical end.

What most students of the art of preaching want to know of one who has long practiced the craft is this: " How do you actually make a sermon? Let me stand at your elbow when you stand at your bench. I concede the importance of the theory and I realize that only as I grasp it shall I understand the reason why you do many things, but, nevertheless, let me watch you at work. How do you prepare to preach? "

The answer to that plea must engage us now.

Preaching involves direct and indirect preparation. Each sermon calls for particular preparation, but all sermons call for general preparation too. If we look at the indirect or general preparation first, we can turn to the particular preparation later.

All life is preparation for preaching. The life of the Christian is a " life hid with Christ in God," and in every

week the devout soul will learn something of how the
Father deals with his child. George Müller wrote a book,
The Lord's Dealings with George Müller, but every Christian has such a book unpublished in his heart. Life for the
Christian cannot be just the passing of time or a succession of events. He is being *dealt with* in events by a pur-
poseful and loving Father. The events have meanings,
therefore. He interprets them, seeks their inwardness, and
learns God's will that way. The man who lives heedless
of God and sees no purpose in events may learn nothing
from life except, perhaps, a few cynical maxims — and
they will be false because he has no spiritual key to experience.

No preaching is great preaching that is not highly informed by a life of Christian experience. A man may be
rich in academic knowledge, and reach with skill for the
exact quotation he wants from modern and classical au-
thors, and urge his whole case with a cogency none can
deny, but if no heartthrob beats beneath it and nothing
he says has been hammered out on the anvil of hard experience, his preaching will lack something which nothing
else can make up. The simplest people will feel the deficiency. They may not be able to *explain* it, but they will
be aware of it. The sermon is clever and, as a work of art,
irreproachable. But they know that another man with half
the ability gives them more help.

Particularly is this true with trouble and sorrow. No
one can wish for sorrow, or go and look for it as a preparation to preach! But, soon or late, it comes to all. God forbid that the preacher should waste it when it comes! Of
all the wicked waste in the world, none is so sad as wasted
sorrow. To pay the price and buy nothing with it! To have
some terrible experience and no enrichment when it is
past!

But if a man finds God in his sorrows and learns how to cling on in the dark, and sees the stars peep through again after total eclipse, and gains some spiritual nourishment from every bitter drop, there will be deep notes in his preaching which even the insensitive will not miss.

Not only will the Christian learn from his daily life with God; he will learn especially from those periods in every day which he fences from all distraction that he may be quiet and alone with God. These are, indeed, the times when life receives its deeper interpretation for him, and when God communes with his soul.

If a preacher has no sustained and secret intercourse with God, if he is under the condemnation of those ministers whom Alexander Whyte mentions as attempting flights of prayer in public of which they know nothing in private, if the slow and costly toil of intercession is all cut out for other things, a dreadful deficiency will appear in his preaching too. It is not only that he can never speak convincingly on " How to Pray," or " How to Want to Pray More," or " How to Meditate," or " How to Be Disciplined in Devotion," or " How to Use a Prayer List " (and a dozen other " How to " sermons of the devotional life), but that something spiritually pervasive is wanting in every sermon he preaches. No one can explain how a healthy soul clothes all its expressions (and even its silences!) in the atmosphere of God, but one is aware of it. One is supremely aware of it in preaching. One feels of some men that they have come straight to the pulpit from the audience chamber of heaven. An awe-filled hush falls on a people whose minister belongs to that high order. They wait in confident expectation. They know it will be a word of God.

To life in its wholeness as lived with God, and to life in its secrecy lived yet closer to him, the serious preacher

adds systematic Biblical and theological study. It is still
not particular study for a particular sermon. He aims to
know all the Book, its highways and byways, its background and foreground, its broad sweep and its detail as
well. He is glad of all helpful commentaries upon it, but
he is rigid in his determination to let no commentary, nor
all of them together, become in his studies a substitute
for the Book itself. He has been warned that it is possible
to know with intimacy many books *about* the Bible and
not know the Bible. He is grateful for the warning. It is
the Bible itself he is resolved to know. He lives in the Book.
It becomes autobiographical to him. He is himself the
leper whom Jesus touches to healing; he is Peter when
Jesus thrusts the threefold question at his heart: " Lovest
thou me? "; he is Paul when he sings with Silas at midnight in the Philippian jail.

He *reveres* the Book. Every scholar is his friend who
makes the Scriptures still more clear. If he has no Greek
or Hebrew himself, he masters the English Bible and compares translation with translation: K.J.V., A.S.V., Wey-
mouth, Moffatt — he knows them all. His respect for the
Book comes out in many ways. He never allows his homiletical desires to engineer a sermon out of a false translation. He would like to preach on the Boy Jesus busy about
his " Father's business," but he knows that the Boy did not
say that; he said that he was in his " Father's house."

On his study of the Bible he builds his theology. His
theology is *Biblical* theology. He believes of God and his
dealings with men what is taught in the Book and what
can honestly be inferred from it. No doctrine commands
his unquestioning acceptance that he cannot find in the
written Word. He leaps no gulf, therefore, when he moves
from Biblical to theological thought.

It is the peril of some ministers after ordination to neglect their heavy reading, but not the serious preacher of the Word. The Bible, theology, apologetics, the philosophy of religion, Christian sociology, psychology, all have their turn with him. However much he has the scholar's heart, his pastoral responsibilities will prevent him from contributing in any large way to the literature on these subjects, but he is determined to keep up with what others are saying.[10] He fights to prevent his study from becoming only an "office." However much the business demands increase upon the modern minister, he is determined, above all else, to be a servant of the Word. He aims at an average of four hours' study a day. It will be less on one day and more on another. Early rising or late sitting (though not both) will be necessary to maintain his standard, but he achieves his end with quiet resolution.

Being a serious theologian, therefore, he exults in doctrinal preaching. He laughs at the idea that it must be dull, and he positively scorns the suggestion that it is unrelated to daily life. Part of his picture of the ideal man in the pulpit is the teacher-preacher. When he falls in with brother ministers who have had three or four years' theological training and who tell him at a fraternal that they have had little use for a great deal of what they were taught at college, he is frankly bewildered. It is a poor return, he thinks, for the consecrated scholars who instructed them, but the men appear to believe what they say. They listened to what they were taught, and can discuss it in theological circles, but it seems never to have related itself to the pulpit. It lies like academic lumber in their minds and they do not know that *every* doctrine can be preached

[10] For a method of storing the fruits of one's reading and how to make a preacher's index, see chapter IV in my *Craft of Sermon Illustration*. It deals primarily with illustration, but the same method applies to the storing of material also.

—not every area of mystery dispelled, but the essential truth made clear. Indeed, it is seriously to be doubted whether any doctrine has been understood if it cannot be preached. Dr. W. Russell Maltby sums up his case against one part of Dr. P. T. Forsyth's teaching on the atonement by arguing that it cannot be " so vital a truth if it can only be expressed in terms quite beyond the reach of a plain mind — in other words, if it cannot be preached." [11] Dr. Dale passed his book on the atonement through his pulpit at Carr's Lane, Birmingham. If a minister were tempted to comment on that by saying that congregations were different then, he would expose himself to the rejoinder that preachers were different too.

Clearly, then, the preacher will be that rarest of men — a thinker. He will not be just a wide reader, peddling other people's thoughts. After his devotions, the best hour of his day will be the hour given to sheer thinking: assembling the facts, facing their apparent contradiction, reaching up for the help of God and, then, driving his brain like a bulldozer through the apparent chaos to order and understanding at the last.

How a man thinks best, only he can tell. Some men think best in utter quietness in their study, some as they walk alone; others must speak their thoughts aloud — to themselves or to a friend. Let a man respect his own preferences here, but let him be sure that he *thinks*. Books may serve to start the current of his thought, as a little water thrown into a pump can create enough suction to secure a steady flow, but his own thinking is the really valuable thing and will mark all his preaching with the hallmark of distinction. To what a high order the thinker-preacher belongs! The literary essayist in the pulpit ap-

[11] *Christ and His Cross*, p. 150. Epworth Press (also Abingdon Press, 1936).

pears puny beside him. The studied elegance and patterned mosaic of other men's thoughts seems fiddling while Rome burns beside the work of one who comes straight from the audience chamber of heaven with an urgent message that has been wrought out in him while he wrestled with God as Jacob wrestled at Penuel. Reality is written over all the man says. If there are times — and there will be — when his message is clearer than others, there will be no times when he is guilty of that superciliousness which some scholars affect toward unlettered people. He will respect profoundly the sheep God has given him to shepherd, and they, for their part, will be grateful that when he cannot show them plainly all he sees, they can at least catch inviting glimpses of the verdant leas to which he will bring them. Of one thing they will be always certain: their pastor thinks with God.

So much, then, for what we have called *general* preparation. It is real because it is life: life in its day-to-day events as lived with God; the secret life of the soul; the strenuous life of the mind. All a man's ordinary education, be it much or little, lies behind this preparation for preaching and serves the pulpit how it can.

Direct preparation is our interest now. The time has come to make an actual sermon. How do we go to work?

It is clear from our consideration of this general preparation that no man goes to work without a thought or purpose in his mind. He is called to preach. The constraint is already on him and the broad content of his message already in his mind.

But what of the actual theme of a particular sermon — the precise delimited aspect of truth that is to be the whole substance of his preaching on one specific occasion? How does that come?

It will come in one of two major ways. *He* may choose *it*, or *it* may choose *him*. It could be either. Let us look at each of them in turn.

Some themes he chooses himself. After careful thinking he can calmly decide to deal with certain subjects that seem to need treatment in his pulpit. He may be aware that there is confusion in his people's minds on those particular themes and he may feel, quite modestly, that he is equipped by life and study to deal with those aspects of truth. He looks ahead through the weeks and months and, if it is his high privilege to speak to the same people week after week, he can plan a sequence of sermons (whether he announces them as a " series " or not). He can thus save the time others lose in wondering each week, " What can I preach on next? " It is all planned. The preacher plans it. He devoutly hopes that God has had his share in the planning too, but, humanly speaking, the initiative and the foresight and the decision are all his own. He may decide in his morning sermons to expound, passage by passage, a certain epistle or a minor prophet. Very good! The plan is clear. The work is straightforward. It is sheer exposition: the elucidation of meaning. It will call for all the linguistic scholarship he has, but whether he is rich or poor in this branch of learning, commentaries will have something to give him. If he is ripe in this kind of scholarship, it cannot but interest him to know what other scholars have thought about it, and if he has none of this stored knowledge, he will depend on the help of commentators all the more.

Consequently, he will have on his shelves the most useful commentaries he can get. He may not have complete " sets " of commentaries. That can be a snare. Any set of commentaries on the books of the Bible undertaken by a team of men is inevitably uneven. In one series, perhaps,

Romans has been done well but Mark is poor. A complete
set looks nice standing on the shelves of his study, but
books to a preacher are tools, and a carpenter does not
much care how his tools look or whether the handles are
all of the same style. He only wants them to be serviceable
for the job.

So with the expositor-preacher. Let him make his own
" best set." It may be The Acts in this series, the Pastoral
Epistles in that, and The Revelation of John in a third. If
a man, beginning to build a preacher's library, were to say,
" But how do I know which commentary is best in which
set? ", a scholar will tell him. Biblical scholars are free
with their help. There is a fair degree of general agree-
ment as to the most successful efforts of commentators.
One must not be a slave to their views even when one has
considered them. Nothing can exempt the preacher from
his own discipline of thought and prayer. But there are
the books, fashioned for his help, and the lifeblood of consecrated men is in them. Differ with them if you must, but
do not differ lightly. Take what you need and go to work
on that expository series. Get the background of the
epistle, and understand the historical setting of the minor
prophet. You need not burden your people with all you
know. What you say at any time will be but a tithe of your
knowledge. Parading scholarship is an unpleasant vanity
in the pulpit. To help the people is your ruling aim. At the
last, you want them to feel how wonderful is Jesus, not
how clever is the preacher, and Dr. Denney said that if
you are aiming to do the latter you will fail with the
former. Relate what you are expounding, where possible,
to the lives of the people in front of you, and make that
epistle, or prophet, or whatever part of Scripture you are
explaining, the very *word of God* to the people who are
sitting before you in the pews.

Or the preacher may decide, not on the exposition of a book, but on a Biblical character study or studies. Again the task is straightforward. Work through the concordance — and be sure that you have a *complete* one. Heap together all that is said about that particular man or woman. Consult a good Bible dictionary, lest you should have overlooked some of the material and lest you should have confused two persons with the same name. Assemble every known fact about the person whose life you mean to examine. Brood over it! What is really illuminating here? Can I best teach these truths this way? Have I enough material? Shall I need to draw on dubious traditions — or traditions of any kind? Is it really important that I get this said? There is often an honest, adequate, and most helpful sermon on men and women of whom little information is given in the Scriptures, but the little is important and enough. Five verses of the Bible are given to Epaphras. Just five! But we learn that he was (1) a faithful minister, with all that that implies when uttered by Paul. We learn that he was (2) a good colleague, a man one could work with. Let no one miss that note of high praise! There are some fine men, even in the Christian ministry, who can work with no one else, and no one else with them. They are individualists and must be accepted with their temperamental defect, and God sometimes honors their separated toil. But it is deficient in certain precious ways. You cannot "lone-wolf it" in the fellowship of the Christian Church and reach a maximum for God. Epaphras did not fail there. He was "a beloved fellow-servant." He was even more. We learn that (3) he "labored fervently . . . in prayers" (K.J.V.). All his public ministry was reinforced with private intercession. He preached and he visited (as most ministers do), but he had this other and lovelier and rarer distinction — he wrestled with God in secret for the souls of the people he served.

All the material for the sermon is in those five verses. Nothing is strained. What is given invites and, indeed, demands expansion. The Bible is full of major and minor biographies. We have looked already at the gains and losses of this preaching. Here it is our simple purpose only to show the way a man may go to work when he has a Bible biography in mind.

Or the preacher may decide neither to expound a book by passages nor to study the life of a devout soul by a Bible biography; he may choose to set the truth out in an analogy lifted from the Scriptures. He may speak of Christ as Light (John 8:12) and find that there is still much unfamiliar material in a comparison that he fancied had already worn thin. Or he may picture the Holy Spirit as fire (Luke 3:16) and ask himself whether there is anything in cold Christians that can really burn with the fire of God. And why not? There is coal in Antarctica! The chill John Wesley found his heart warm within him in a little room in Aldersgate Street.

> " O that in me the sacred fire
> Might now begin to glow . . . ! "

Or he could visualize the Saviour as a sure Foundation (I Cor. 3:11) and find several sermons in that one analogy. He could discuss " The Necessity of a Good Foundation," or " The Qualities of a Good Foundation," or " The Dangers to a Good Foundation." Each is a sermon. All the material is there. Browsing in books on building, and brooding on what one finds, offers rich analogical stuff. He may have known nothing before of natural subsidence, or the peril to buildings from coal and salt mining, or the dangers that arise from covered streams, but, as the facts take order in his mind, they suggest rich comparisons in the Christian life and the dangers to which the best foundation is exposed. The analogy need never be strained. As he returns constantly to the central comparison for fresh facts, his people find the sermon not only matched to their spiritual need but crammed with sheer interest as well.

The Christian as salt (Matt. 5:13), both as preservative and condiment (!), or hope as an anchor (Heb. 6:19), or the prophet as a lamp (John 5:35) — Bible analogies tumble over one another in their number and suggestiveness. Let the preacher mark his course in handling them with reasonable care. He must avoid, on the one hand, the trite, and obvious, and childish comparisons and, on the other, those odd, bizarre, and detailed identifications that some men make just in order, it would seem, to be different. Between those two extremes there is plenty of deep water. Sailing confidently there, the preacher will bring many a rich cargo to his people's eager minds.

Perhaps a man is seized with the conviction that he must give a series of sermons, not to the expounding of a book, or a set of Bible characters, or a succession of analogies, but to a doctrinal task. He may decide to take the Apostles' Creed, or the Lord's Prayer (treating it theologically rather than devotionally), or selections from the Westminster Confession of Faith. Again, the work is straightforward. He must make theology palatable. He will not come to his work with the arrogance of a dominie who says, " They've *got* to like it," but with the zest of one who knows that, once the attention is fully turned that way and once its overwhelming importance is understood, it is truly fascinating in itself. Not for nothing has theology been called " the queen of the sciences." Not in pride, but in bare truth, did the theologian say that every problem at the last came to him. " I will prove that to my people," says the teacher-preacher to himself. " I will make them *extra* glad whenever I take a doctrinal sermon in hand."

All this preaching is clearly *planned*. It avoids the dangerous " hand-to-mouth" method in the pulpit: the recurring uncertainty of what to take, and the lack of any kind of sequence or comprehensiveness in the preaching of a whole year. It would surprise some ministers, if they examined their sermon records, to discover what important subjects have received no attention at all, and how their own moods, and even their whims, have affected the choice of their themes. In whatever other ways we approach preaching — and those other ways we have now to consider — it is imperative that a man so plan his work that in the passing of the years all aspects of truth receive attention, and the central truths of the faith not only attention but stress.

Sometimes the preacher does not choose his theme: the theme chooses him. A text may confront him and say, "Preach on me," or a theme may bestride his path and demand to be dealt with. Many of our finest hours in the pulpit come in this way. Seldom do we feel more sure that the word is " given."

Every serious preacher has a notebook in which he notes these texts when they arrest him, or these themes that insist on being heard. He puts them down instantly or, at least, within the hour. They may come in his devotions (when " what to preach" is most definitely *not* in his mind), or in his pastoral work, or in his general reading, or in conversation with a friend. The whole sermon does not usually come in a flash (though even that occurs now and then), but the text or theme comes clearly and a light comes clearly on it too. It gleams! A facet of truth sparkles in his eye and seems to say, as it shines before him, "Hold this up for your people to see." Put it down at once! — the text or theme, with a phrase to indicate what you saw in that gleaming moment. Let it lie there in the notebook with many others, *each on its separate page*, and, once a week, turn over the leaves of this most useful book. Few books that repose upon a preacher's desk are more important than the book in which he garners these flashing thoughts.

It might be worth a moment to picture this book a little more clearly, seeing that it is an indispensable aid to those who would be expert in the craft of the sermon. The masters of our craft think of the book under various metaphors. Some of them think of it as a greenhouse and their deposited thoughts as cuttings; some think of it as a great shipbuilding yard, with many vessels in various stages of construction standing on the stocks; some think of it as an incubator containing many eggs. The metaphor does not matter. So long as we picture something in building, or in cultivated growth, it will serve. Some preachers — Moody, for instance — dispense with the notebook and substitute large envelopes (one envelope for a theme) that they may poke in, not only their own developing thoughts, but any relevant newspaper cuttings as well; but that substitution of means is a detail — the method is the same.

Among the many merits of this method of early preparation is the opportunity it gives to God to guide us farther in our preparation, and the opportunity it gives to the subconscious to work upon the subject too. Six hours at a stretch on sermon preparation is less valuable than three periods of two hours each. The periods when the conscious mind drops the theme are valuable too. The subconscious mind does not drop it. It works on while we turn our thoughts to other things: it works on in sleep; it gathers and compares and ferrets around for half-forgotten facts; and when we turn our conscious mind to the subject again, it throws up valuable and partly digested material and seems to say, " Is this of any use? " Turn over the pages of the notebook once a week. Look at each theme in turn. Some will grow more quickly than others. New thoughts will come in this casual looking. Put them down instantly on that same page in the book. The time has not yet come for the most serious work upon the subject, but cuttings in a greenhouse must be watered and the hull of a ship must be sound before the launch. Give the seed thoughts attention and watch them grow. In due time their hour will surely come.

It may be said that one cannot " adopt " a method of sermon preparation that depends upon ideas coming of themselves, and this, in a sense, is true. But one can adopt and cultivate a sensitivity to such ideas and an attitude of expectant quest. It is not a worried pondering: " What can I preach on next? " — one may have a full deliverance from that fearfulness — but it is an attitude to life and work that recognizes that the chief responsibility is God's and that, if one keeps open to him, the ideas will flow in. It is quite unimportant at this stage whether the gleaming flash comes as an idea or as a text. So long as it comes with the preaching imperative in it, respect the inspiration of God, and give it a page in the book. By so doing you will be saying to your subconscious: " Here is a subject. Hunt around for me in the files of my mind," and while, of course, the fruit of that subconscious searching will depend in part upon how much is already in the files, it cannot fail to bring something of value to serve the high purposes of God.

The day for direct work upon the sermon will surely

come. Anticipating next Sunday's preaching, on Tuesday the preacher will turn to his book and pass the pages before his eyes. On one of those themes his mind will fix. Sunday morning's sermon is a planned Biblical exposition maybe; this is for the evening. As his eye falls upon a certain page and he glances over the notes he has added with passing time, something will say inside him, " Its hour has come." The text or theme " chose " him when he first put it down, and it chooses him again in this important moment. Lifting it out of the book, he lays it on his desk and the work begins.

Observe that he is not starting with nothing. Already he has something highly valuable here. Text or theme, he puts it down upon the top of a sheet of paper and, with his garnered thoughts already written in the notebook before him, he begins to brood. He gets his mind under way: " What is this saying to me? What must I say about it? " He bores into the heart of the subject. If little comes from his first hard thinking, he turns up the text in a commentary, or consults any notes he may have on the general theme. But he is careful not to read too much at this stage, and unshakably firm in his resolve not to read a sermon by a master preacher upon the same text. Experience has taught him that this latter course will overwhelm his mind and make his own budding thoughts seem worthless in comparison. *He* is the preacher. It is God's word through him that the people await. His reading in notes or commentary at this stage is just enough to get the engine of his own mind turning over or (changing the metaphor) just like the jugful of water we mentioned which gets the pump working once more. Soon he quits reading and broods again. With mind open to God, but bent on the theme, he concentrates. He knows that the disciplined mind can almost get into a coma of concentra-

tion. He wants to reach that spot where he is unaware of
his surroundings and alone with God and this word. Over
and over in his mind he turns the central thought. He tries
to split it wide open with piercing questions. He may, indeed, approach it with the familiar interrogations: "How?
Why? When? Where?" — though they may only chip the
surface. Presently he sees the inwardness of it all. One
ruling question thrust at its heart and the thing is in pieces:
natural, workable, proportionate pieces. Another stage of
the sermon has been reached.

He begins to put thoughts down upon paper — any
thoughts that come and in any order. He tumbles them
out, the good and the not-so-good. Another sheet of paper!
Down they go until the flow has ceased.

"What have we here?" He goes over them again. It is
a mixed bag, but the truth he wants to utter lies somewhere in this jumble. He questions his own mind.

"Can I now say clearly what I clearly want to say?
What is the *one* thing I mean to get across? I must chisel
a phrase. What shall it be? Could it be this? or this? or
this? No! *That is it!* I'll write it down and fix my line.
Up with a fence firmly drawn around that theme! Nothing
must creep in that is really outside the fence. No fringe
stuff either! Much that I have written here must be ex-
cluded. Into the bin with it! One thing I do, and nothing
shall deflect me from that central purpose! Here is my
fecund phrase! There is my fence! I know what I want to
say. I know it is important. How can it best be said?

"Let me think of the congregation! There are the students in the gallery and the grand old folk downstairs;
there are the lonely women of the middle years, and those
fine workingmen who are so regular in coming; nor can
I forget the small but important professional group. With
all of them in mind, how can I best put this over? Shall I

argue it from beginning to end — even if I argue in reverse? Is it best dealt with by faceting, or does it categorize with naturalness? Shall I cast it all into one strong analogy? Whatever I do, I must not rush the preparation here. No polish can redeem bad structure, any more than new paint can save a jerry-built house.

"Actually, it could be handled two ways. I could argue it and make it a chain of logic from beginning to end, or it could be worked by facetry. Which is best, subject and congregation both held in mind?

"On the balance, facetry here. It could include argument in subsections, but one piece of sustained argument is not compelled by the theme and, after all, the congregation is not all made up of students. Moreover, I seem to glow over it more when I visualize it treated by faceting. To get the glow in preparation is so important; that inward thrill at the prospect of proclaiming the truth seems to well up again in the actual proclamation itself. And what of the psychological method? It may be authoritative or persuasive — but, almost certainly, persuasive here.

"Very good! Another sheet of paper! Text at the top. If I have begun with a subject, I must have it linked up now with the Book of God. The theme — my pregnant phrase — underneath. On what pattern shall I facet? My aim is really the buttressing of faith. Clearly, therefore, I should facet on the pattern: *This is true because.* . . . What, then, are the facets (or headings)? It is true because: (1) . . . (2) . . . (3) . . . (4). . . . Which is the best *order* of the headings? Number 2 is stronger than number 4 and really sequential to it. Change them over! I must build up, of course, to a climax. The light ought to fall full on that fine face at the last.

"Good! This is a strong structure. Maybe I should turn up some books again now, and think out the matter for each heading. Each section must be well paneled in and I must get an idea just where the joints should come; one must not 'bump' at transitions, but plan to run over with smoothness. A well-chosen metaphor will often do it. It can be flung out like a hook from one section of the sermon and picked up by a complementary hook in the next.

"How would it be best for the whole sermon to *begin?* Does the context offer a striking beginning? Is there an opening sentence in the news of the week? I need not stay in the newspaper more than a moment. Or shall I leap over someone else's back with a short, memorized, and apposite quotation?

"All in all, it must be the context here. Honesty and full understanding demand it, and it need not be dull. I can arrest by the very surprise of the setting.

"What about the conclusion? It is not 'how to.' I am nourishing faith. Success here is marked by the people's complete assurance of the truth. On the whole, it is a time for recapitulation. I will hold the jewel up at the last for a further look, and turn it so that the facets catch the light again in quick succession, and I'll drop the curtain suddenly with the light full on that central face.

"Fine! It is going well. Another sheet of paper for a full and ordered outline: Text. Theme. Opening. First heading, second, third, fourth. Conclusion. Space beneath each. I must put in still more work on these sections. Each is a minor whole in this faceting structure, with its own beginning, development, and intermediate conclusion.

"Where should the illustrations come? At the beginning, perhaps, of point one. It will picture the whole thing, and I can focus my aim best that way. Also under point three, which will be thick and shadowed if I do not light it up.

"It is a good outline. I can start writing now. Yes! Every word of it must be written from beginning to end.

If I write a sermon a week for ten years, I shall have a terse, clean, direct style which will benefit all my extempore speaking. Nothing now but the sheer labor of writing, and it is all a labor of love. Let me be quiet with God before I begin. Let me be sure that this is, indeed, 'a manifestation of the Incarnate Word, from the written Word, by the spoken word.' Perhaps I should leave the writing until tomorrow, for God to correct or confirm what now seems so right for me to say. Unless I meet unexpected difficulties, four good hours after this stage should see the sermon done. I have something good for my people next Sunday! "

Let me give an illustration of this method actually at work even though it be (for the sake of variety) different in structure from the one suggested above. I turn over the pages of my notebook and see a page headed with the text: " At home with the Lord " (II Cor. 5:8). A note reminds me that it is the American Standard Version rendering and belongs to a passage in which Paul sighs for heaven. I see that I have added different thoughts and queries on various occasions when I have turned to this page in my book. "He longs for heaven but, earth or heaven, he wants to be with the Lord. But heaven is his *home*. Home! — lovely word — perhaps the sweetest in our tongue. What makes heaven home?

> " 'Thy presence makes my paradise,
> And where Thou art is heaven.'

Is no man at home until he is with the Lord? Is a man really lost away from Christ? Does he know it? Is there something in men that witnesses to a royal origin? Is our racial memory only of sin?

" Let me brood on these notes. There is stuff here. On

to the desk with it! I will wrestle with this theme and make a sermon now.

"Paper! Text at top. Let me think! What is it saying to me? What aspect of it do I really want to get out? It is not a plain expository sermon. I am going to 'convert' the text into a theme. But what? Does my preaching imperative center in 'home' or 'heaven' or in the human heart? Where is the focal point at which my concern and that text meet?

"Home? Is it home? But that might lead me away to the praise of earthly homes. Very nice, but not my concern now!

"Heaven? Is it heaven? But I cannot give a map of heaven, and I must not be lost in vague imagery or sheer otherworldliness.

"Over and over in the mind it goes. I begin to write: scraps of this and that; all related but no sure line yet. I turn it about this way, that way. *Why* does he want to be at home with the Lord? *Where* would he be at home with the Lord? Only in heaven? Not here? *How* is a man at home with the Lord?

"There are several possible themes here, but one is beckoning me on; something is struggling for expression through that text and my soul; something *particular*. I've got it! Of the many things here, this is what I want to consider — the reminiscence of God in the soul. Is there such a reminiscence? Am I foolish? Am I in danger of speculating about the soul's pre-existence? What is it that I want to say which is Scriptural, experiential, and practical too?

"I want a phrase that will state my title and fix my fence. 'The Appetite for Heaven'? No! 'The Echo of God in the Heart'? No! 'The Homesickness of the Soul.' What about that? That's it! That fixes the line. Away with all this stuff about our earthly homes; no maps of heaven either; never mind, at this moment, about Paul's wanting to be off. I fix on this alone: 'The homesickness of the soul.' Anything in the commentaries about this? No! Pity! But they are concerned, quite properly, with sheer exposition. I have 'used' my text for a theme.

"Let me think of the congregation. The youth will laugh up their sleeves if I talk about heaven. Or will they? The hardheaded businessmen will think I am sadly irrelevant today. Or are they hungry for a sure word? I can make them *all* see the relevance of this. It will lead me to dig in their own souls, but people do not really mind one mining there. Vanity, perhaps! But I am as guilty myself. *Is* there a homesickness of the soul? What is that passage in Wordsworth's 'Intimations of Immortality'?

> "'Not in entire forgetfulness,
>   And not in utter nakedness,
>   But trailing clouds of glory do we come
>   From God, who is our home.'

What did Cleopatra mean when she said,

> "'I have immortal longings in me'?

It means more to me, I fancy, than it meant to her. Or Charles Wesley?

> "'With songs to Zion we return,
>   Contending for our native heaven.'

'Return . . . our native heaven'!

"Now I must decide on a structure. Can I prove that there *is* a homesickness of the soul? that we are only at *home* when we are with the Lord? that there is a reminiscence of God in all men?

"It must be argued, of course — and out of experience.

But what is the evidence? Not *very* weighty, surely? I will build on two facts verifiable in experience: first, that there is something in man that earth can never satisfy; secondly, that there is in man a nostalgia for heaven. The psychological method must be persuasive; the illustrations will have to be fairly free and, therefore, brief. I am glowing over this already. It will, at least, be unusual today to have a sermon on heaven!

"Another sheet of paper! Text. Theme. Two major headings.

"How shall I begin? I know! The homing instinct of birds and beasts and fish. Fascinating stuff there. Mention eels! Nothing more wonderful. It can all be brief and I will challenge them with this, 'Is there a homing instinct in man?' I shall then be right at major point number one.

"How shall I conclude? I want them to recognize, respect, and nourish the reminiscence of God in the soul. There must be some 'how to' in this, but it will probably strike home best with a good illustration that summarizes it all.

"I think I am ready now for the full outline. How can I make those two major points really strong? The first is not so hard. Nothing on earth *does* permanently satisfy. I can prove that. Neither money, position, fame, pleasure, nor rude physical health. They only *seem* to satisfy, and that only for a while. Earth satisfies the beasts; it cannot satisfy man. What does Browning say?

"'Irks care the crop-full bird?
    Frets doubt the maw-crammed beast?'

William Watson knew that earth could never satisfy. He asked,

"'In this house with starry dome, . . .
    Shall I never feel at home?'

I can prove all that, and nail it home with manifold illustrations; indeed, I shall have to be careful to see that the
illustrations are kept in check.

" But the second point, viz., that there is in man a nostalgia for heaven? Can I prove *that*? I have got Wordsworth and Charles Wesley lined up, but I do not want
too much poetry even if it is familiar. Can I prove it from
the plain man? I think I can. He also has immortal long-
ings in him. Erskine of Linlathen will serve me, and Logan
Pearsall Smith in reverse!

" I shall have to face the fact before I conclude that this
will all seem ' otherworldly ' to some of the congregation,
but I do not fear that. I know that only those people work
with full effectiveness for the New Jerusalem below who
clearly see the New Jerusalem above and who aim to
make it after the pattern that God showed them in the
mount. I will give them a pointed reminder of the glorious
social consequences of the work of John Wesley, Lord
Shaftesbury, William Booth, and other God-intoxicated
men, all consciously marching to Zion, all sure of heaven.

" I am ready to write now, but I have done enough,
perhaps, for the day. It wants to be prayed over and left
to lie fallow. I will write it tomorrow — and it will be fun.
There is nothing irreverent in feeling that way about my
work. My people seem to enjoy hearing what I enjoy in
preparation; and they not only enjoy it — they translate it
into life."

It might be felt by some students of preaching that the
practice of writing every sermon out in full is unnecessary
labor, especially to a man with a natural gift of fluency,
and it would be honest to admit that some slight peril does
attach to the rule. If a man make the habit so slavish that
he cannot even " thank the ladies for preparing the tea "

without writing his words out first, it has become an awful prison. But the commoner danger — and especially with those who are naturally fluent — is to rely upon their gift of speech; and, because they do not write, they develop a diffuse style full of " hedging " adjectives, and they always seem slow in coming to a conclusion.

My own practice in the early years, when I was usually facing the same congregation twice a Sunday, was to write out one sermon fully and preach the other from brief notes behind which was no manuscript at all. By writing one sermon a week I hoped for precision, clarity, and terseness in expression; by preaching a sermon without writing every week, I hoped to develop the freeness and readiness of the true extempore style. Each method helped the other. The people never knew my methods, nor could they have distinguished any difference in the preparation by the preaching. The passing years bring a greater mastery of the craft, and a man will probably feel less and less the need to write in full. He may choose to write only the beginning and end of his sermon and, perhaps, the more closely reasoned parts of his argument. A word on the manuscript suffices for an illustration, and terseness is attained without the sacrifice of spontaneity. It is the man who has never written his sermons out, and never intends to, who is almost certainly doomed to unconscious repetition and mediocrity. Without being aware of it, he constantly repeats himself in ideas, in illustrations, and in phrasing. He seems incapable of letting his nouns appear in company alone. He tries to disguise the paucity of thought by piled-up adjectives. At his best he is rather repetitive, and at his worst he is a windbag.

It needs hardly to be said that, because a man writes a manuscript in his study, he is not compelled to read it from his pulpit desk. On the contrary, one greatly hopes that he will do no such thing. It is folly to suggest that no readers were great preachers. Some most influential ministers of the gospel have read their sermons to the people. Thomas Chalmers read — not with the adroitness of Dr. J. H. Jowett, who was barely known to be reading at all — but with his finger on the line and his nose near the paper. Yet his sermons were mighty! The Holy Spirit can inspire a man in his study and with his pen in his hand, as well as a man in the pulpit with nothing written out but a few notes.

Nevertheless, every preacher should aim to be free of his manuscript, and not too tied to his notes. If you have got something from God to say to the people, it is better to look them in the face when you say it. The people normally feel about a man who reads his sermons that they get his message without getting " him." Something of the easy commerce of pulpit and pew is sacrificed in this way. A man is not so open to those sudden inspirations which a preacher often feels in the act of preaching and knows, in the very moment of their reception, that they are given from above. Nor can a pulpit reader easily defer a point that he is making if, momentarily, something disturbs the congregation and he wants to get them settled again before he nails the truth home. He is on car lines and he must run to the end of his track.

The practice of writing the sermon in full, coupled with warnings against reading it in the pulpit, is not a circuitous way of advising a preacher to learn it off by heart. It would be better to be a good reader in the pulpit than a preacher who consciously memorizes. For one thing, no man sustaining a constant ministry to the same people could do it, and, for another, it has most of the disadvantages of the read sermon in addition to placing such a strain upon a man's mind and nerve that it is almost cer-

tain to break him in some way, as it broke Morley Pun-
shon years ago. A man who writes his sermon out, and
reads it over two or three times before delivery, unconsciously memorizes parts of it. No harm in that! But the
point to bear in mind is this: he is not *trying* to memorize
it. He faces the people with his mind filled with his message and he aims to clothe his thoughts in fitting words
just as the message unfolds. The gains of writing the sermon out are not shown chiefly in that particular sermon
but in the style of *all* his preaching — the extempore
preaching that has a manuscript behind it and the extempore preaching that has no manuscript at all.

For men of unusual temperament, or nervous apprehension, no rules can easily be laid down. One must just
be grateful that God owns sincere and prayerful work
howsoever it is offered to him. But for the majority of men,
and especially for those in their prentice years, this seems
the best advice to me: no conscious memorizing; no reading in public; write the message out in full when you can,
and then lay the manuscript aside; take notes, if you need
them, to the pulpit — as few as possible; lift up your heart
to God, look the people in the face, and say the word he
has given you to speak.

" How long should I preach? " is a question one is sometimes asked. It is a more difficult question than appears on
the surface. It really relates to *how* you preach. Ten
minutes is too long from some men, and thirty from others
leaves one longing for more. I went to morning worship
years ago in the English Church at Ostend. It was a gray
November day and I was hungry for the company of my
fellow countrymen and as prepared for worship as I know
how to be. God was there! — and perhaps nothing else
matters, but the sermon at that service has always stayed
in my mind: the sermon as a fact, I mean; nothing much

about it. The text was an obscure verse from Ezekiel and
was more obscure when the sermon ended than when it
began. It was " confusion worse confounded." It was counsel darkened with words. I was surprised afterward to
realize that it had been going on only for seventeen minutes: it had seemed an age. Yet I have heard Dr. F. Luke
Wiseman and Dr. C. Ryder Smith (not to mention others)
when fifty minutes seemed like five. When

> " Heaven came down my soul to greet,
> And glory crowned the mercy-seat."

Not only does the length of the sermon depend on how
you preach; it depends also on the subject. Bishop Stubbs
of Oxford told the curate who asked him what to preach
about that he was to " preach about God and preach about
twenty minutes," but, excellent as that advice is in some
ways, it ignores the fact that in the variety of subjects
with which a preacher has to deal there is a necessary
variety of length. Some subjects are adequately dealt with
in twenty minutes; others require forty. If you have mastered the craft of holding the people's attention, and if
they know you well enough to understand that the sermon
is always as short as an adequate dealing with your selected aspect of truth allows, they will not resent the extra
time when you require it.

When the sermon manuscript is finished, it must be
checked — checked by the preacher himself. That is yet
another gain of writing out in full what one means to say.
Criticism of a sermon *after* it is preached, whether the
criticism comes from a man's own mind or from his wife,
comes (so far as that occasion is concerned) too late. The
sermon has been preached. That is why dramatic criticism
in newspapers is limited in its usefulness. It also comes
too late. The play is on before the critic sees it. The only

hope one may have from the most informed and helpful
criticism is that it may benefit a man's subsequent work.

But if a preacher prepares a full manuscript, he can
check it himself before its delivery. Suppose he fixes his
themes for the following Sunday on Tuesday and has the
sermons finished by Friday night: one in outline only,
and one fully written out. He has part of Saturday, at least,
for his final preparation. Included in that final preparation must be a drastic examination of what he has written,
with questions like these in mind:

Is the subject big enough? It might be thought that any
subject that a man chose to deal with in the pulpit, and
that had a link with the Bible, would be " big " enough
for preaching, but it does not necessarily follow. Some
men have an itch for out-of-the-way texts, which often
lead them to trifling and out-of-the-way subjects. One has
sometimes suspected that there was a vanity in the choice
of the odd text and the hope that the people would wonder, " Whatever will he get out of that? "; and, if that were
true, it would be low indeed. It is better to take the " big "
texts, even though one feels inadequate before them, and
something of a failure afterward, than petty things easily
understood and not much worth understanding at the end.

Does this sermon do one thing well? It is a common fault
of unpracticed preachers to have too much in their sermons or, at least, not to be loyal to the one theme they
have ostensibly chosen. If they have enough of our craft to
put a fence around their theme, they had not had, alas!
enough firmness to respect the fence. Unrelated, or tenu-
ously related matter, has been admitted. Consequently,
directness has been lost. The unity of the sermon is not
obvious. It could not wear Paul's phrase as an honest
motto: " This one thing I do." The sermon comes to its
conclusion, but no one could say at the close precisely

what it had set out to achieve. In reading his sermon over
before delivery, therefore, the preacher will question his
mind particularly about that.

Is there something in it for most people? It is possible to
make a well-wrought sermon, and on an important subject, but important only to a few, or important to people
who are not there. We have already glanced at the folly
and danger of denouncing the sins of people who do not
come to church, but the whole error is not compassed by
that. I preached a sermon once on scrupulosity, and it may
have been intended by God for someone. But, in the hour
of preaching, a sense of the rareness of the sin in the modern world (whatever may have been true of the ancient
monastery) came over me, and I felt that the subject
would have been better dealt with in private talks to the
unusual men and women who suffer from it, or, if in public
preaching at all, not as the theme of a whole sermon but
simply as the subject of a section. The point of a sermon,
therefore, should not be too fine. It should be calculated
to meet the needs of more than a very few.

Has the subject overlaid the object? Sermons, as we have
seen, have both a subject and an object. Normally they
are knit together, and the subject, well handled, achieves
the object as its end. But, curiously enough, it is possible
for the subject to work against the object, and it happens
this way. A man can become self-consciously clever with
our craft. He may take an artist's delight in sermon structures, in the balance of parts, the smoothness of transitions, and the variety of illustrations. To achieve professional competency and please his artistic taste, he may
forget that the real end of the sermon is a spiritual object.
It happens, sometimes, that the spiritual object may require some sacrifice of literary skill and homiletical artifice.
The practiced preacher will have that especially in mind

when he checks his own manuscript. He must sometimes throw away devices that please him by their deftness in order to thrust more directly at the vulnerable spots in the hearer's heart. Preaching was never meant to be an opportunity for human self-display. The sermon has a work to do. It will be judged, not by its artistry, but by the effectiveness with which it does the work.

The Marquess of Reading (then Mr. Rufus Isaacs, K.C.) was once defending Mr. A. G. Gardiner in a libel suit. He virtually won the case; a farthing damages was awarded. When the jury had given their verdict, Gardiner warmly thanked his astute advocate, but said: " Mr. Isaacs, why did you alter your line of defense? You never touched our real case."

" My dear sir," said Isaacs, " his lordship is a plain man who loves a plain issue. Your real case was complex and would have tired him and irritated him." [12] That was how he had won, with judge and jury as well. He checked the impulse of his fine mind to deal with legal finesse *in order to win the case*. The preacher must win the case. Whatever militates against winning the case is his enemy — even though it be his own skill!

Is the matter in this sermon in the best order? It is surprising what effect order can have upon the worth of one's material. To alter the position of a point in a sermon is often to vary its value enormously. In one place it can be smashing; anticipated too soon, or arriving tardily, it might almost as well have been thrown away. One develops an extra " sense " for judging order. It is splendidly fostered by the discipline of logic, but even without that one grows in ability to say of a point in a sermon: " There is its place. That place! — that, and no other."

Is the style simple, nontechnical, and non-Canaanitish?

[12] A. G. Gardiner, *Prophets, Priests, and Kings*, pp. 156 f. Dent.

The simple Saxon word is always to be preferred to the classical polysyllable, except when meaning is at stake. Even then a Saxon *phrase* might be preferable to a word of Latin origin that the people only dimly understand. Although this rule can be overpressed, it is normally true; the nearer to the soil, the nearer to the people.

One cannot, of course, avoid using words of both origins, nor should one try. The two main streams that pour into English enrich our tongue, and it would be a foolish and unnecessary impoverishment to deny ourselves the use of both if we always bear in mind a preference for the simpler. Indeed, a preacher is driven to use both, if only because he is compelled by his work to say the same thing over and over again, and yet keep the topic fresh. More than most men, therefore, he is in need of synonyms. Yet it remains true that he must always prefer the simpler word when he can find it. Everybody will understand him then; a speech compounded of unusual and unexplained words will leave many people lagging behind.

But even men whose normal style is simple get into the way of overusing, in the pulpit, the technical language of theology. That it must be used on occasion none can doubt. How can the teacher-preacher make any headway at all if he be forbidden to speak of reconciliation, redemption, atonement, salvation, sanctification, and a host of similar words? Use them he must sometimes, but they all want minting afresh for the modern congregation, and no man should use them lightly who is not certain, and certain by his own clear and reiterated teaching, that his people *do* understand what these great terms mean.

And, if the preacher must be careful today not to overuse the technical terms of theology in preaching, must he not be even more careful about the use of technical terms from psychology, which are uglier than the theological

terms and have no ancient and high warrant in the Book
of God? Preachers often speak today (and without explanation) of phobias, traumas, complexes, apperception,
schizophrenia, primordial, subliminal, etc. All these words,
no doubt, have their proper place, but it is seldom in the
pulpit and perhaps never without explanation. And the
number of words one can stop to explain is very limited
in the course of a sermon which is setting out to do something else. In most cases, it is possible and better to change
the word.

Nor do these end the stylistic blemishes the preacher
looks for as he checks his sermon. He looks also for " the
language of Canaan." Deeply read as he is in the Bible,
and warmly attached to his hymnbook and to the books
of classical devotion, he finds that their phrasing (archaic
now to modern ears) has crept imperceptibly into his own
style and, whenever he writes (even for the secular press),
he finds himself writing " parson's English." It is not a very
serious fault in the pulpit. The people who hear the
preacher know and love the language too. Every community has its own characteristic speech, and there is a
mellow beauty about the language of Canaan. The words
seem soaked in the devotion of the centuries.

Nonetheless, it is sometimes perplexing to the young
people, and it is certainly perplexing (if I may employ a
bit of it in uttering the warning) to the stranger within
the gates. "Outpourings of grace," "the witness of the
Spirit," "washed in the blood," "toiling in rowing"—
four phrases that I heard recently in one religious address,
and a hundred similar phrases, mean very little to the
people outside and whom we are particularly eager to
interest when they make their infrequent visits to church.

Consequently, when the preacher examines his manuscript, he does so with a pencil in his hand and he prunes

his style of everything which will hinder understanding in the people he longs to win.

Other things he will bear in mind also in this final revision: the number and adequacy of the illustrations, the power of the sermon to grip quickly, the clean, direct way it comes to its end. The checking will all be done with his heart lifted to God, and his mental eye upon the people. He trusts that God will own the word and say of this also: " It shall not return unto me void, but it shall accomplish that which I please, and it shall prosper in the thing whereto I sent it."

Well! There it is! The sermon soundly made, the manuscript written, and the manuscript checked. It has been hard but happy work. There is no way of taking the toil completely out of it. Every sermon takes its toll of hours, and *must* do so. Work in the study; work as one walks; work, maybe, in the trains. But it is done now! Read it again. Make a few notes. Away with the manuscript. The time has come. Lift your heart to God for a crowning blessing on the word which he has given you, and which you have steeped in prayer from the moment it came, and go, with ambassadorial humility and authority, and give it to the people.

VIII
Mistakes Commonly Made

WE HAVE had need in every chapter, as we have come to it, to utter certain warnings against the dangers that beset the preacher's path. Every legitimate subject of preaching, every structural type, each of the psychological methods is prone to certain weaknesses, and we were at some pains to point them out. The beginnings and the ends of our sermons were in need of warning words as well, and it has been our simple strategy in this book not to tie the preacher too closely to rules but to point out on each part of our voyaging what was the Scylla and Charybdis of our course. " Keep in the deep water between those dangerous extremes," we said, " and you are safe."

It is necessary, before we conclude, to touch lightly on some common mistakes already mentioned, and then to mention certain others that have not come under our notice until now.

It is imperative that the preacher shall not himself lose faith in preaching. If a man suspects that that dire catastrophe has happened, or is happening, in his soul, let him regard the discovery with something of the horror he would feel at a clinical confirmation of cancer in his body. Let him solemnly face the fact before God that it will eat his life away. Let him recognize that it can grow to size

and strength in such secret ways that he can be all unaware of its power until it is fatal. Let him aim to live so
near to God that he is made aware of the earliest beginnings of this deadly disease, and made aware, also, of the
way to a cure.

Confidence in preaching is not so very hard to maintain.
It is largely a matter of one's devotions. If a man is vigilant
here, if he keeps his appointments with heaven, if he
treasures up the proofs which God gives him of the power
of preaching (his own or another's), and if he remembers
clearly what someone's preaching did for him in his youth,
he will not slide into supposing that it is a useless and
parasitic occupation. When he thinks on all that God has
done by preaching through the years — Gregory of Nazian-
zus, Chrysostom, Ambrose, Bernard of Clairvaux, Wycliffe,
Hus, Bossuet, Richard Baxter, George Whitefield, Jonathan
Edwards, Spurgeon, Hugh Price Hughes, and tens of
thousands of lesser known men — he will not wave it aside
as " sound and fury, signifying nothing."

So regarding it, he will not allow related occupations
to squeeze it from its fitting place. Living as a minister in
the modern world, and admitting the need to take his part
in communal affairs, he will not permit anything to lessen
his reverence for the pulpit, or prevent his making the
most thorough preparation to " administer the Word."

Acknowledging that some men have special aptitude
for the work, he will not allow that anyone is more
" called " than he is called himself, or that anyone has a
finer gospel to proclaim. The same commission and the
same gospel given to Chrysostom are given to him. If, by
nature, he is not so " goldenmouthed " as that prince of
orators, he is determined, by the help of the Holy Spirit,
to bring what has been given him in nature to the highest
pitch of perfection that he can. The idea that hard work

is unnecessary if you have the Holy Spirit, he spurns for the lying laziness which he knows it to be. Without the divine blessing upon it, he is aware that his work will be vain, but he knows also that he cannot expect the divine blessing unless he has done all that he can himself. Laying his best work before God, he is bold to say, " This is my utmost, Father; now add the power which thou alone canst give."

Nor does he try to be original. He recognizes that he has an *old* gospel to proclaim. He exults in its age. It is the same gospel brought by the apostles. It has met the needs of the faithful for nigh two thousand years. It must be stated freshly and in the thought forms of his own age, and lighted up, no doubt, by modern instances, but the longing to say something no one has said before he recognizes as a snare to avoid.

Nevertheless, he is determined never to be *dull*. One can be interesting without being " original." It is a harder and higher task to make the old and true winning and meaningful than to make people gasp at bizarre " originalities." Deeply he believes that preaching ought to be interesting. It is astounding to the natural mind at all times that God should commission any order of men to be the mouthpiece of his will but, once allow that possibility, and it is incredible that the communications should be dull. There are times when the preacher can only give his *own* views of certain matters he raises. He has no clear word from the Lord. But, normally, it is not views he brings but *news*. It is surely one of the most incredible of all things that news from God should not only be dull at times but expected to be! Against that the preacher resolutely sets his face. Whether the people bear or forbear, it will, at least, be a thrilling announcement as, like an eager herald, he publishes it in the face of all men. To those, even of his own order, who deny that preaching was meant to be interesting, he can but say, " I do not believe you."

Curiously enough, the idea has gone abroad in some quarters that it is scholarship that makes preachers dull. The idea is ludicrously absurd, but it is not without interest to inquire how the belief got abroad.

Some men parade their scholarship. They are not, as a rule, the riper scholars, but industrious hacks who display the worst fault of " academics." Having become more interested in books than in life, they grow less and less able to clothe their ideas for preaching in the experiences of common men, and need to turn more and more to tomes for the stuff of their sermons. Consequently, much of it is secondhand and has a musty smell which normal persons dislike. These men are in danger of becoming mental recluses, out of touch with life, and this robs their preaching of any chance it ever had of being real.

Yet scholarship is important. Books are precious tools. The minister who neglects his Greek, for instance, has thrown away a master key. No man who preaches can ignore an opportunity for learning. The chances of wider education for some laymen who serve the pulpit may be few and far between, but it is all the more important that they seize what chances they can. But no man in the pulpit ought to parade his learning. Carry it lightly! If ignoramuses think you have no store of erudition because they can " understand everything you say," and think it is all so simple because you take pains to light it up with illustration, let them think it. The preacher has his own temptations to pride, and everything that keeps him low before God is to be welcomed. Yet be as learned as you can. Be *accurate in your learning*. Be a *specialist* in something — even though it be but a fragment of all you would like to know. I knew a lay preacher once who specialized in the

book of The Acts of the Apostles. It was not the substance
of all his preaching, and I discovered his specialism only
by accident, but my heart warmed to a man who worked
long hours for the bread of this life, yet gave all his leisure
to the service of the pulpit and, as one secret side line, had
made himself master of a book of the English Bible. Much
of it he knew by heart. All that the chief commentators
had said he knew also. He had the humbleness and exact-
ness and reverent curiosity that great scholarship always
wears. Lightfoot and Westcott and Moffatt would have
owned him a brother, I think. It was only early depriva-
tion that had so stringently narrowed the range of his
research.

If a preacher approaches his work in a spirit of awesome
reverence for God and for his truth, he will never despise
his hearers or fall out of sympathy with the common people. There are ministers who — half unconsciously, no
doubt — despise the people they serve. " If I really let myself go," they seem to say, " if I told them all I know, how
could they understand it? It would go clean over their
heads. Nor do they want the best I have to give. The mass
of people do not come to church at all, because it is entertainment they want, and the few who do come look for
entertainment even in the house of God. I will not pander
to them."

I cannot think that Jesus would speak or think like that.
Though he said that the way to life was narrow and " few
are they that find it," he did not despise the people. He
had compassion on the multitude. He never hardened his
heart against the people who were looking for happiness,
and looking in the wrong place. It is difficult, perhaps, for
a preacher who has faithfully offered the bread of heaven
for years without response to " maintain the spiritual
glow " and keep a tenderness in his heart to the people
who ignore him and may even treat him as a joke.

But he must do it! The moment love for them leaves his heart, and deep solicitude for their salvation goes, he is finished. The preacher at a seaside resort makes his way to his almost empty church and sees a vast unheeding multitude spilling over the beach and not caring a bit that it is Sunday; the preacher in town makes his way to church and sees the railway stations and bus stops crammed with trippers and hikers, who have no interest whatsoever in the things he lives to declare. It is hard for both these unwanted men not to lose faith in their calling and not to despise the people in their hearts.

But they must win that victory. The warm overtones of love; the proper deference which arises from honest respect for human personality; the accent which only genuine caring can put into a man's voice — all these are necessary if preaching is to have power. One cannot despise or patronize the people and succeed in winning them. It would be a pity if one could. The gospel of love can hardly be effective on the lips of men who haven't got it themselves.

On all these points we have lightly touched in our earlier study. Upon a few others of varying importance it may be useful if some stress is placed before we conclude.

1. *Don't apologize for the sermon as you begin*

It sometimes happens that when a man has done his best in preparing a sermon, it seriously disappoints him even when it is complete. This is deeper than the common experience of feeling that the sermon is not "perfect." That will be a normal judgment of the preacher on his work because, as a craftsman with ideals, he will always have it at the back of his mind that his best sermon has not yet been preached.

But, occasionally, having done his best in prayer and

thought and sheer unhurried work, the thing does not "come out" as he hoped. It has never taken fire in his heart. He has checked the importance of the theme, the soundness of the structure, the adequacy of the illustrations, and the clean directness of the conclusion, and yet he feels unsure of its power even as he goes to preach. The temptation to apologize as he begins may enter his heart.

That temptation must be resisted. The expectation in people's minds (which is always present, in some degree, as the sermon begins) is a precious asset of the preacher, and to smother it with apology and begin by implying, "I have nothing much for you this morning," is among the most foolish things he can do. He needs their interest and expectation all the more on an occasion like this. The work has been honestly done. What guilty unbelief in God has convinced the preacher that the Holy Spirit will not honor the sermon at the time of its delivery and "send the fire" even as it falls from his lips? To douche the warm hearts of the people with cold water by way of introduction is the poorest way to start a fire ever devised by the vanity and unbelief of man.

Nor is this advice less good when the time spent in preparation has been inadequate and, for reasons beyond the preacher's power, the work has *not* been well done. To the man who scamps his work by sheer laziness or inefficiency, or because he is a hireling and not a shepherd, or because he puts golf before the gospel, or has no faith in his message or love of the people, I have no word to say. The bitterness of his remorse in eternity, when he faces at last all the consequences of his sloth, will be in itself (I imagine) almost more than he can bear.

But there are, now and then, more respectable reasons than these for coming to the pulpit inadequately prepared. An epidemic may have swollen sick visitation to most un-

usual proportions. The preacher may be unwell himself,
or have serious sickness in his own family. Quite inescap-
able problems of administration may press upon him with
peculiar heaviness in one particular week. For these good
reasons — good enough to be given to God — the preacher
comes to Sunday and knows that his messages are not
adequately prepared.

It is still wise not to apologize as one begins. God gives
extra help to men who toil terribly at all times but whose
toil at this unusual season could not be directed to pulpit
preparation. Let a man be open with God in such an hour.
Let him look his Father in the face and say, " I have done
my best with all the time I had." It is enough! God will
undertake! No apologies! Go in full reliance on the Holy
Spirit and the people will be blessed.

During the Second World War I lived in air raid shelters
in London for more than five years. I had no books but the
Bible, and no real privacy day or night. At the periods of
intensive attack, the work among the bombed-out people
was so exhausting that one lost all sense of time and often
did not know, in those underground caverns, if it was
Tuesday or Thursday, eight o'clock in the morning or
eight o'clock at night. One just went on and on, snatching
an hour or two of sleep when the needs of the people
abated a little, and then getting up and going on again.

Yet Sunday came round with the same regularity, and
I had to meet my much-tried people, many of whom had
lost their homes and some of whom had lost their dearest,
and all of whom were in sore need of the bread of life.

I never went to my pulpit less homiletically prepared,
yet never with greater confidence in God and the word I
had to give. My sermon record assures me that I never
fell back on " old stuff." God undertook! " Give them this,"
he said. He gave me the message, and immense confidence

in it at the same time. The hungry sheep looked up and they were fed.

In normal days the times of inadequate preparation come rarely in a disciplined preacher's life. When they do come, fling yourself on God and make no apologies!

2. *Don't be inaudible*

However rich a man's message may be, it is no good if it is not heard. People complain constantly that the preacher is inaudible. Sometimes there are wrangles between the pulpit and the pew as to where the fault really lies.

Churches are often bad acoustically. Cruciform and domed buildings, in their different ways, can distort a good voice. Some deaf people insist on sitting at the back and then putting all the blame upon the preacher. " Why do deaf people sit at the back of the church? " someone asked a well-known minister. " Because they are not only deaf but daft," he answered tartly. But he was *too* tart. We must be tender toward the deaf, who often come to worship with faithful regularity and sometimes hear so little. The wisest of them sit forward and it is very rewarding to see the gratitude in their faces when we succeed in making them hear.

Passing the blame, however, from pulpit to pew, and pew to pulpit, is no way forward. The chief responsibility rests unquestionably on the one whose task it is to lead the worship and to preach. He believes he is bearing a message from God. The necessity to make the people hear should burn in his heart.

Sometimes the pew gives advice to the pulpit on elocution, though, as a rule, it is not very clear advice, and interesting only in that it proves that the people are not hearing. They tell us to speak *naturally*, which is telling us nothing at all because the word "natural" is a rough and undefined word at any time, and what is natural to one man is not natural to another, and no man who spoke "naturally" would be heard at the back of a large and echoing building. The "conversational style" in preaching has its merits for those people who like a sermon to be "a little intimate chat between you and me," but nothing accounts for the inaudibility of the pulpit more than the popularity of the conversational style. It is sheerly *not* suitable for most large churches, and a herald is not having an intimate chat with anyone but proclaiming a message from his King.

This question of style in preaching, therefore, seems deeper than the ordinary person knows. It turns on the very conception of the preacher's office. If preaching is the sharing with other Christian friends of "a few thoughts that have occurred to me," a conversational style and a half-apologetic manner is fitting, but, if a man believes that he has come from the presence of God with an urgent message to men, he must *proclaim* it without a trace of apology, and you cannot proclaim in the conversational style. When one digs into the minds of people on this matter, one does not find them unwilling to receive a proclamation. Indeed, they rather like it. The too tentative preacher with his deferential ways distresses them. "If you have a message from God, let us have it," is the language of their hearts. It is pomposity they dislike in a preacher — not the manner of the herald — and that runs deep into the question of a man's own secret commerce with God.

Another common piece of advice the pew often gives the pulpit is this, "Don't drop your voice at the end of a sentence." If the advice were strictly taken, it would make nonsense of half we say. Of course, one must drop one's voice at the end of a sentence, but the drop must be in *pitch* and not (if the people are to hear) in *volume*.

It will be clear from this that a preacher can learn much that is useful from those who teach voice production and elocution, but he must be sure that he is in the hands of a sound teacher. Some men have been damaged by elocution lessons and have made their message still harder to receive by oversyllabication, and emphasizing the *little* words, and so stressing their final consonants that they add another syllable to almost every word they speak.

Nor need we ask our teachers of elocution to iron every trace of the county of our origin out of our speech. That Dr. W. E. Orchard grew up in London and Dr. J. H. Jowett in Yorkshire was traceable in their fine preaching, and the preaching was no worse for that in either case. That some breath of our native heath is still about us is a far less serious fault than that we should appear affected in the pulpit. A teacher of phonetics went to prayers some years ago at a council school in the East End of London and heard the Cockney children sing, " Prize Him for His grice and fiver." On the following Sunday, he went to worship at a church in Mayfair and heard the little choir boys exhort the congregation to " Preese Him for His grease and fever." On the balance, the phonetic expert preferred the East to the West. Though both were shocking, he thought the former sounded " more real."

Good, clear speech is our aim, and no fastidiousness. Above all else, *be heard*. Spurgeon, with his fine voice, was impatient of the people who used him, either way, for their examples in elocution. " Listen to what I am saying," he said. " If you were listening to a will being read, you would not be studying the lawyer's elocution. You would be too concerned to learn whether or not you were a legatee."

3. *Don't preach* at *or* under *or* over *the people, but to them and* for *them*

Some men earn the reputation of being pulpit scolds. They seem, all the time, to be in a denunciatory mood. They denounce the general world situation, the sins of statesmen, the sins of society, the sins of their own city, and the sins of their own congregation. They do it, moreover, with detachment, as though they were not themselves in the world, the state, society, the city, or the local church.

It is a pity. We have already noticed that it is spiritually debilitating for people constantly to hear sins denounced that are not their own. But it is not spiritually nourishing if, when they go to worship, the preacher seems always to dwell on the faults that he is so expert in finding in his people themselves.

There are moments, no doubt, for denunciation, but no man should enjoy them. Frankness should not exclude tenderness. The task should hurt and be seen to hurt. The preacher should not exclude himself from condemnation. I may not be guilty of drunkenness or lechery, but I belong to the society in which others have found it easy to go that way — and into that way, but for the grace of God, I should have gone myself.

Moreover, life is hard: burdens are heavy; sorrows are bitter. People need encouragement and comfort.

Don't talk *at* them.

Don't talk *under* them.

Some men treat their congregations like the intermediate department of the Sunday school. Their sermons are children's addresses. They pause to explain simple words. Their whole manner makes it clear that they rate the intelligence of the people very low.

It may be admitted at once that the average congregation is not deeply read in theology or philosophy. It must be admitted, also, that the Bible is not so well known as it used to be. It is clear also that in any congregation of reasonable size the educational level will vary, and the preacher must have regard to the people whose minds move more slowly than the rest. But none of these admissions nor all of them together justify a preacher in treating an adult congregation as a set of juveniles or a collection of morons. Those people have learned from life if not from books. It insults their maturity to be treated as children. Most of them will understand the hardest things if the preacher will explain them and take time to light them up.

Don't talk *over* the people.

This is the commoner fault. It is not hard to understand how ministers slip into it. Many, many years of their life are given to the study of spiritual and ethical problems. Things that were complex to them as students have become simple and familiar with passing years. They fall into the way of supposing that those same things are familiar to their hearers. They make statements that presume a knowledge or a viewpoint the people do not have. Unless the minister keeps close contact with people in their normal lives, and cherishes at least one pagan friend, he will begin to live a life dangerously apart from his fellows. His very goodness may insulate him. I heard a minister say once in a class meeting that he was ashamed to confess that it was only with difficulty that he could maintain his four periods of devotion a day. It was said humbly, I believe, for he was a good man and conscious of failure. But several of those who heard him found it hard to say their prayers unhurriedly *once* a day, and the good man's confession discouraged them beyond measure. " I haven't even begun this life," they were mistakenly tempted to think.

Don't be too obviously *over* the people in learning or devotion either. A leader must not be so far ahead that the people who are following cannot keep him in clear view. A leader *belongs*. He is kin. A minister is identified with his people in seeking and finding, in success and failure, in disappointment and achievement as well.

So when he preaches, he preaches *to* them and *for* them. One feels it all the time. Love wells out of him. He *cares* for the people. Their help is clearly his whole concern. Nothing matters to him in this half hour but that they grasp the truth, or feel the love of God, or taste and see (as he, himself, most obviously has done!) how gracious the Lord is.

Some men conduct worship and preach with a certain detachment from the people. It is not clear that they are themselves worshiping. They seem to give a hymn to the people and then wait for them to finish it. It would appear that they are serving the meal but not eating it too. Some subtle identification is lacking.

Perhaps that identification comes only of supernatural love and has to be received, like so much else in the ministerial life, on one's knees. But it *can* be received! It puts a wooing note into all one's appeals, even into one's warnings. It makes one careless of many things and certainly of one's reputation as a preacher. With Paul, one feels:

> " O to save these! to perish for their saving,
>   Die for their life, be offered for them all."

4. *Don't steal other people's sermons*

Plagiarism is a nasty sin. It would be nasty in anybody, but it is doubly nasty in a preacher. What kind of ethical sensitivity has a man who takes somebody else's work and passes it off as his own? From a man set apart to divide the word of truth it is dishonorable indeed.

The heartiness of our condemnation makes it necessary, however, to be plain what we mean by " plagiarism." A man is clearly no plagiarist (literally, abductor, kidnaper) who takes a sermon and tells his congregation from whose volume he has taken it. No congregation or author would resent that on rare occasions, especially if the sermon expounded some difficult theme and the preacher felt unequal to the subject himself. Nor is a man a plagiarist who seeks stimulation for his mind from the work of other men. In that sense of the word Shakespeare would be a plagiarist. So many of his stories are borrowed; the lustrous garments are all his own. To cut a piece of cloth off another man's roll is not, I think, a sin in literature of homiletics, but to steal the suit that he has made and parade it as one's own is plain theft. The robber might as well have put his hand in our pocket and taken our purse.

Years ago I was on holiday at Tighnabruaich in the lovely Kyles of Bute. I went to worship on the Sunday evening and sat under the ministrations of a visiting preacher. When he announced his text, I was arrested at once, having preached on the same text myself two or three weeks before. I was still more arrested when he began with a flat contradiction of the text — as I began myself. Word for word my sermon came out — just as it had appeared in a verbatim report from a religious journal which had published it without permission. The central illustration was a personal experience of mine. He gave it as his own. My children sitting beside me in the pew remembered the sermon and looked at me in astonishment. I blushed for the cloth. If I had been preaching in the pulpit a week later and had repeated my sermon, *I* should have been suspected of plagiarism.

But that salutary experience taught me something else. Nobody can steal like that and really make it his own. The whole thing lacked a certain conviction. *It wasn't his!* The experience he was describing had not been beaten out in his own life, and he said things I had learned in sorrow as though he was mildly inquiring of someone's cold in the head. On his lips that message did not do the work it was made to do. He was not behind it. If there were no ethics involved in plagiarism, it would still be a thing to avoid. One secret of power in preaching is to know the truth of what you are saying and believe it utterly. There are senses in which everyone can say with Paul, "*my* gospel," for there is something of himself in every message the preacher honestly prepares. You are false, and you *feel* false, when you steal another man's message and offer it as your own.

5. *Don't repeat your own sermons unless you can glow over them*

A preacher may repeat his own sermons when he is preaching in another place, and would be wise, on occasion, so to do. Some men think it is dishonoring to God not to prepare a new sermon every time they mount the pulpit steps, but that is a rule that I find unconvincing. Having blessed the message to one congregation, God can bless it to another.

The only peril a man is in who constantly repeats a sermon is that he will go on repeating it when it has secretly ceased to thrill his own heart and fails to kindle within him as the word of God should. Men who are always itinerating, or take short pastorates and work each time through the same set of sermons, are most guilty of this sin. And it is serious! It really prevents God from saying through them the word the people most need to hear. Sermons date in odd and subtle ways. The preacher's own spiritual growth, one would suppose, demands that he throw aside those outworn garments. Surely he has learned something new of life and of God since he shaped that message years ago.

Moreover, it is only constant and fresh work in sermon preparation that keeps the life in preaching. If it does not seem new and wonderful to the pastor, it will not seem new and wonderful to his flock. The gospel does not change with changing years, nor yet the heart of man, but let a preacher beware lest he use that as an excuse for failing to seek the latest bulletin from heaven and go instead (like some itinerant evangelists and some ministers in the middle years) with an address dropping with age and curiously unreal even to himself.

When a man repeats a sermon, let him rethink every bit of the argument; let him inquire how its relevance can be made plain in the very hour of its utterance; and let him drop it the moment his heart has ceased to glow.

6. *Don't imitate other preachers or envy their gifts*

It is not surprising, perhaps, that young men whom God has called to preach and who feel unequal at times to their high calling should envy men who seem able to do the work without strain, and who go on doing it year after year. They may envy their voice, their range in language, their felicity in illustration, their power in argument, their gestures, appeal, and personal presence.

It is best to put all that out of one's mind. We do not possess those gifts, and we must accept ourselves. We can put no other man's gifts on the altar, only our own.

Our own are dear to God. He knew what we had, and had not, when he called us, and he means to give his message through our consecrated personality. We shall not try, therefore, to be anybody else. Conscious imitation will only make us ridiculous, and not that only: it will hinder God in using what we are in ourselves.

We shall not even *envy* other men their gifts. In the mercy and by the miracle of God, we may have things they have not got. Let us be ourselves — our *best* selves. We will pray and work, and work and pray, and dare to believe that the God who called will equip us and speak his word through our unimpressive personality and faltering lips, and choose again " the weak things of the world, that he might put to shame the things that are strong."

7. *Don't preach without preparing your own heart*

Preparing to preach is not the same as preparing a sermon. Preparing the sermon is only part of the preparation. A man must prepare himself. That is why it is unwise to leave the preparation of the sermon so late that one is feverishly working on it almost up to the hour of its delivery. Inevitably, there will be something of breathlessness and haste about that message, and, probably, something of breathlessness and haste about the messenger too. And that would be sad! We live in a breathless world, but God forbid that flurry should invade the pulpit. The preacher's whole demeanor should partake of the calm and joy and serenity of God, and none of these is ever successfully faked. The peace of God's house, the awe of his worship, the wonder of his presence, cannot be simulated. If they are regnant in the preacher's heart, they communicate themselves to the congregation. The preacher need not *say* it. The discerning know that he feels it:

> " Lo! God is here! let us adore
> And own how dreadful is this place! "

All this comes in the preparation of oneself. The hour is approaching when I must conduct worship and preach the Word. The sermon is made; lessons and hymns are chosen; my mind and thought are ordered and ready. I need another equipment I cannot get myself. Let me be quiet before God. Let me carry the people I must address to him. Let me admit my nervousness and shrinking in the face of this task. Let me confess my unworthiness to bear any message from heaven. And as the Holy Spirit helped me in the preparation, let me expect him in the pulpit also.

I bow in silence at Thy feet.

"Woe is me! for I am undone; because I am a man of unclean lips, and I dwell in the midst of a people of unclean lips."

"*Lo, this hath touched thy lips; and thine iniquity is taken away, and thy sin forgiven.*"

Forgiven greatly, how I greatly love!

"*Whom shall I send, and who will go for us?*"

"HERE AM I; SEND ME."

"*Go*"!

Index